Bryan Grimes, Pulaski Cowper

Extracts of Letters of Major-Gen'l Bryan Grimes to his Wife

Bryan Grimes, Pulaski Cowper

Extracts of Letters of Major-Gen'l Bryan Grimes to his Wife

ISBN/EAN: 9783337147365

Printed in Europe, USA, Canada, Australia, Japan

Cover: Foto ©ninafisch / pixelio.de

More available books at **www.hansebooks.com**

EXTRACTS OF LETTERS

OF

MAJOR-GEN'L BRYAN GRIMES,

TO HIS WIFE,

WRITTEN WHILE IN ACTIVE SERVICE IN THE ARMY
OF NORTHERN VIRGINIA.

TOGETHER WITH

SOME PERSONAL RECOLLECTIONS OF THE WAR,

WRITTEN BY HIM AFTER ITS CLOSE, ETC.

COMPILED FROM ORIGINAL MANUSCRIPTS
BY PULASKI COWPER,
OF RALEIGH, N. C.

RALEIGH, N. C.
EDWARDS, BROUGHTON & Co., Steam Printers and Binders,
1883.

PREFACE.

The matter contained in the succeeding pages was never intended for publication. It represents a short sketch of incidents, and participation in the late war, by the late MAJOR-GENERAL BRYAN GRIMES, and extracts from letters to his wife, written from the camp, and on the fields of battle, and such other matters of record and interest as have seemed to me fit and proper to be inserted therein.

GENERAL GRIMES had for years after the surrender determined to write out his recollections of the war, solely for the benefit, pleasure and curiosity of his children and their posterity, to be read in after years, with no view whatever of their publication, but simply to be kept as a matter of record in his family. He had commenced this work, as shown in his original manuscript, and, as far as executed, it is printed in the following pages.

In his letters to his wife, he gave briefly an account of what almost daily transpired, and being written on those respective days, was fresh in his recollection, and may be received as strictly authentic. His known integrity and truthfulness will need no corroboration of what he has written or related.

These sketches and incidents demonstrate the character, honor and chivalry—the obligation of duty, and love of country, of a true citizen and a brave soldier. They present a truthful and impartial history, and will be read with interest and gratification by his friends and surviving comrades in war, and with this view they are thus publicly presented.

It will be observed that in one or two places disconnected notes appear, indicating clearly his intention to refer to them at some other time, and to extend more fully their subject matter. I have thought proper to have them printed just as they appear, and as they are written in the original manuscript.

It will also be seen that mention has been once or twice made of his horse "Warren." His affection for this animal was very great. He had been released from all work since the war, except now and then his own occasional riding, and the best attention had been given him. I have frequently heard him say, that however much he might need the money, he would not part with him for thousands of dollars in gold. This old war horse died only a few weeks ago, at the age of twenty-eight, and in accordance with the General's known wishes, was buried as carefully and as decently as a human being near the spot where his dead master now rests.

MAJOR-GENERAL BRYAN GRIMES was born in the county of Pitt, on the south side of Tar River, about eight miles from the town of Washington, N. C., on the 2nd day of November, 1828. He received a good academical education, and entered Chapel Hill in June, 1844, and graduated in June, 1848. In about a year after leaving college, his father gave him the plantation upon which he lived up to the time of his death, and whereon his family now reside. He had no desire for political life, and with the exception of the few days he was a member of the Convention of 1861—known as the Secession Convention—he led the quiet life of a farmer, combining industry and good judgment, from his early manhood to the close of his life.

He was on the 9th day of April, 1851, married to Miss Elizabeth Hilliard, daughter of Dr. Thomas Davis, of Franklin county, who died on the 7th day of November, 1857. The only living issue of this marriage is a daughter, the wife of Samuel F.

Mordecai, Esq., of Raleigh, N. C. On the 15th day of September, 1863, he was again married to Miss Charlotte Emily, daughter of the late Hon. John H. Bryan, of Raleigh, N. C., who with eight children now survives him.

My relations to GENERAL GRIMES forbid me to speak in such extended terms of praise as my feelings would dictate to speak of one of the truest and bravest of men. For honesty of purpose—for devotion to principle—for firmness of friendship—for honor in all things—for truthfulness in all things—for faithfulness to all promises and obligations, and for true, genuine courage, he stood on the day of his death the peer of any living human being.

On Saturday evening of the 14th of August, 1880, while returning from the town of Washington, when at Bear Creek, within two miles of his home, he was, just at sut-set, shot from an ambush by a concealed assassin, and almost instantly killed. A little boy, about ten years old, a neighbor's son, was his only companion, to whom he said, "I am shot and will die," and immediately thereafter fell slowly to the foot of the buggy and expired. Several buck-shot struck the ribs and the top of the buggy, but only one shot took effect on his person, which passed through the thick part of his left arm, and lodged deep in the heart.

That evening's sun, just sinking into darkness, left its frowning shadows upon this terrible deed. Its morning rays fell upon a household saddened by affliction, and saw the mother and her children still bending over the lifeless form. Its midday brightness, on the succeeding day, rested upon the large and solemn assemblage gathered at the homestead to render the last and only tribute of respect and affection. The end was soon over, and the tomb received all that remained of him who would have made any sacrifice to maintain his honor, and who did freely peril his life for his State and for his section.

The rounded mound marks now, and will continue to mark, the resting place of one who, in life, bore the type of God's highest creation—the attribute of a Creator's mightiest perfection,

"An honest man the noblest work of God."

To the living and the dead of the Fourth Regiment of North Carolina State Troops, who so gallantly served the Confederacy in the Army of Northern Virginia, the following lines are fitly dedicated.

PULASKI COWPER.

Raleigh, N. C., April 9th, 1883.

EXTRACTS OF LETTERS

OF

MAJOR-GENERAL BRYAN GRIMES.

An account of his own recollections of the War, and a brief account in part of his own participation therein, by the late MAJOR-GENERAL BRYAN GRIMES, taken from his original manuscript.—Extracts taken from letters to his wife from the fields of battle.—His own account of the last fight at Appomattox.—General Orders.—Reports.—Other interesting matter, &c., &c.

I returned from Europe in the middle of the great political excitement over the election of Lincoln to the presidency, and about the time of the secession of South Carolina from the Union, and became deeply interested in the action of the South; and upon the bombardment of Sumpter by Beauregard, had gone down there for the purpose of witnessing the fight, but was too late to see the capitulation.

Thence I went to Montgomery, the then seat of government, and from there to Pensacola, to witness the threatened attack of Bragg at that point. After remaining there a few days, and seeing no prospect of the bombardment, I visited New

Orleans, and came up the Mississippi river to Tennessee, and was on the train with the first troops sent from Alabama to Richmond, and happened to occupy a seat immediately in front of Andrew Johnson, afterwards President of the United States, and then heard the first groans given in contempt of his treachery to the South, which wires repeated at every station, when it was made known that he was on board the train.

On returning home to North Carolina, I found myself a candidate for the Convention which had been called by the Legislature during my absence, to which Convention I was elected without opposition. The election was on the 13th May, and I proceeded at once to Raleigh, and signed the Ordinance of Secession on the 20th May, 1861, and whilst a member advocated the most extensive war measures. In a short time after the organization of the ten regiments of "State Troops" raised for, and by request of the Confederate government, I was offered by Gov. Ellis the Lieutenant-Colonelcy of the 8th Regiment, or the majority of the 2nd Cavalry, or majority of the 4th Regiment, which latter I accepted. I felt my deficiency of a knowledge of military tactics, and Col. Geo. B. Anderson, a graduate of West Point, was Colonel of the 4th Infantry, whilst the others were officered by inexperienced civilians like myself, and I preferred a subordinate position with an efficient officer, to higher rank with officers without experience. In consequence of this appointment I resigned my seat in the Convention and revisited my home for three days to arrange my business matters, and then reported to the commanding officer of my regiment, which was organizing at camp, near Garysburg, where the regiment remained drilling until ordered forward, July 20th, 1861, to Richmond, to be in supporting distance to be called to Manassas in case of need, and arrived at Manassas 29th July, 1861, a few days after Bull Run and Manassas fights, when the change of habits induced a serious attack of sickness.

I received permission to visit the Bull Run mountains to recuperate. After a short absence I returned to my command, and remained with the regiment until the evacuation of Manassas under Gen. Jos. E. Johnston in March, 1862, then in command of my regiment, as Col. Anderson was in command of the post of Manassas and the troops in that section. Camped on Clark's mountain, near the Rapidan river, until April 8th, when the command was ordered to Yorktown, which point was reached on the 9th. Accompanied Col. Anderson when he reported to Gen. Rains for duty, and after assignment to certain posts, civilian like suggested to Gen. Rains that the regiment be not divided for duty as he instructed, but kept intact, and a smaller regiment placed where these posts were intended, not wishing to be left in separate command, the Lieutenant-Colonel being absent.

Here for the first time I became acquainted with the fire of the enemy and was assigned the post of commander of the picket line which I sustained until the evacuation on the night of the 3rd of May, when I was left in charge of the picket line of infantry, with instructions to keep up as usual the firing throughout the night, and retire about dawn, which was very perilous, as torpedoes had been planted on all the roads and streets leading into Yorktown, and my picket had to be kept outside of the enemy's fire. About the middle of the day I regained my command, and encamped with them near Williamsburg for the night, and next day asked leave of absence to visit the venerable institution, "William and Mary's College," during which visit the fight commenced, and carried off by the excitement, I followed the sounds of strife until in the midst of the battle, and never realized my danger until I saw several officers and couriers of Gen.

Johnston killed, thinking that there was no great danger so long as I was no nearer the strife than the commanding General, it then being a prevalent idea, which was afterwards exploded on our side, that the General officers never occupied posts of danger. Seeing the flag of my regiment advancing, I rode up to go in with it and remarked to Col. Anderson, "I hope you have not required my services." And then in the only severe and abrupt manner used towards me before or after, I was informed that my conduct was unmilitary, and my proper position was with my regiment.

The participation of the 4th Regiment in this battle was slight, and the Brigade Commander being placed in command of the field of battle, the command of the Brigade devolved upon Col. Anderson and that of the regiment upon me, when Col. Anderson remarked that he would take advantage of my knowledge of the field of battle, I having been present during most of the engagement and knew the localities, and thus riding over the field we continued together until near daylight, when we were withdrawn. This night, though in May, was one of the most disagreeable of my army experience, a heavy penetrating mist, nearly freezing the men to the bone, when all would huddle together for the mutual warmth of their bodies, and when my horse became the centre for the regiment, around which they collected, the first few attracted by the animal heat from the horse's body, until they formed a complete mass of men.

From thence the army retired slowly, but always on the alert, to the Chicahominy river. While there by an alarm of the approach of the enemy, the tents were all struck and wagons sent toward Richmond, leaving the army tentless and comfortless in the midst of a cold drizzling rain, when taking possession of a rice-tierce, or hogshead, which I shared with Col. Anderson, I became perhaps the most comfortable of all that host, as all comfort goes by comparison.

I was then ordered with the regiment near Richmond, and ordered to report to Gen. Garland, Col. Anderson being in temporary command of Featherstone's Brigade, and withdrawn and returned to Col. Anderson in time to participate in the battle of Seven Pines on May 31st, 1862, which engagement I entered into with 25 officers and 520 non-commissioned officers and privates. All the officers were killed or wounded except myself, with 462 men killed and wounded. I attacked the fort and redoubt where my horse's head was blown off, and falling so suddenly as to catch my foot and leg under the horse. The regiment seeing me fall, supposed I was killed or wounded, and began to falter and waver, when I, still penned to the earth by the weight of my horse, waved my sword and shouted forward! forward! Whereupon some of my men came to my assistance and pulled the horse off, when seeing the flag upon the ground, the flag-bearer and all the color-guard being killed or wounded, I grasped it and called upon them to charge! which they did, and together with others captured the fortifications. Here John Stikeleather, from Iredell, (Company K, 4th N. C. State Troops), came up and requested to be allowed to become the standard-bearer, promising to bear it with credit to himself and the regiment so long as strength and life lasted. After a few moments the enemy began to rally in rear of their tents, and upon my calling Gen. Garland's attention to the fact, I was ordered by him in Col. Anderson's absence, to take possession of a wood near by, and begin firing upon them. In double-quicking across an open space of arable land to get to the cover of these woods, I perceived that the enemy were engaged in throwing up an earthwork to my right, when giving the command by the right flank I charged the works taking many prisoners, and fired upon the enemy for the remainder of the day. That night I slept between Gen. Garland and Col. Anderson on one horse-blanket and covered by another, surrounded by dead and wounded, both men and animals.

The next day was not actively engaged, but retired that night, the enemy having been heavily reinforced. From then until the 26th of June there were daily skirmishes along the lines, when on that day we passed the Chicahominy, near Mechanicsville, and although not actively engaged, was held under terrific infantry fire, and commanded to support other troops and artillery, and remained in that position until near daylight, when we were ordered off to report to Gen. Hill by his special orders. Whereupon he directed me to "charge that battery," which was the only obstacle on the road to Cold Harbor. Whereupon I asked Gen. Hill if he was aware that I had no officers, and only about sixty men, when I was told to hold myself in readiness to charge, if others who were ordered forward a second time failed to take it. I deployed my men on the line and instructed them to fire upon any of these troops who failed to move forward to the charge. They were then successful but found other impediments further on, whereupon Gen. Hill determined to accomplish his purpose without further sacrifice of life, and by a circuitous route caused them to abandon their position, and then marched us down to near Cold Harbor, where we again found the enemy in our front, whereupon Gen. Hill, seeing a battery and not being positive whether they were Jackson's men expected at that point or the enemy, ordered a flag forward to be waved, when I took the flag of the 4th regiment and galloped my horse towards the battery, when they opened with the whole battery on the line in column, in my rear, and here I was on the extreme left of the long continuous line of battle and kept the enemy in check, until late in the afternoon there came an order to charge! and forward they went. My horse was killed and I continued on foot, driving the enemy from. his breastworks through their camps, taking their artillery and supplying myself with another horse. Here I captured a fine St. Bernard dog, which was protecting the corpse of a Colonel of a Pennsylvania regiment, who upon inspection was found to have on steel breast plates, which had protected him so long as his face was to the fire, but upon retreating had received a mortal wound in the rear.

This dog ("General") became the pet of the regiment, and remained with it for over two years, when in pursuit of Hunter in the Valley of Virginia in 1864 he succumbed to the hard marching, broke down and was lost, not having the endurance of men. That night heard the rumbling of wagons and artillery and the tramp of troops, until in the morning it was found that the enemy had crossed the Chickahominy. Here, for the first time, I had the honor of being introduced to the great Jackson, and I now have the mess-chest upon which he joined us at dinner, dining from the contents of a sutler's wagon captured the day previous.

Crossed the river at Grapevine bridge and pursued the enemy as far as the White Oak, when against the consent and protest of Gen. Anderson, who had been made Brigadier, I was detailed by Gen. Hill to take charge of the captured stores and prisoners, and report at Richmond with them. Gen. Anderson saying "that although small in numbers Colonel Grimes and regiment is the keystone of my brigade." I remained around Richmond until about the middle of July, when an attack of typhoid fever compelled me to visit Raleigh and recruit my health. My visit home was of short duration, returning in time to the army to take a part in the first invasion of Maryland and the battles previous to the crossing of the Potomac.

I recall the circumstance near Savage Station of a man perfectly rigid in death, with his musket up to his face, and in the act of taking aim; burning of the trains—pile of metallic coffins—Catholic Priests—a Federal soldier claiming exceptional kindness on account of his being a native of North Carolina, &c. My command did not participate much in the battle of Second Manassas, but were in the field and assisted in driving the enemy beyond Centreville, when the line of march was taken up for Maryland, and reached Leesburg 4th September, and on the 5th, when crossing the Potomac at White's Point, near Edwards' Ferry, I received a very severe hurt from the kick of a horse, which incapacitated me from active duty, not being able to either walk or ride, but had myself carried in an ambulance in anticipation and hopes of a speedy recovery. Here we were encamped near Frederick City for several days, and then moved up to the vicinity of Hagerstown. On the 14th of September the command was called upon to proceed down the turnpike to Middletown, near the pass over South Mountain, when seeing an engagement with the enemy was inevitable, I had myself placed upon my horse and took the command of my regiment, and was first sent with the command to the left of the turnpike, and subsequently withdrawn and ordered with another regiment to proceed to the assistance of Gen. Garland, then engaged on the right. In advancing was met by the corpse of that gallant officer being brought off the field. Here the fight continued all day. Here my horse was killed under me on the mountain and to my own and the surprise of my command I commanded my troops in the battle until nightfall, when I threw myself down to rest by my brigade commander, Gen. G. B. Anderson, who seeing me so exhausted after the excitement of the day, insisted upon my going to the rear, and called up four litter bearers and had me carried to the hospital, upon reaching which I encountered a new danger, as the enemy were threatening the wagon trains, and in consequence as a matter of safety the wounded who were able to be moved without danger were ordered to be transported across the Potomac at Williamsport, where a few of the enemy's cavalry intercepted a portion of the train and turned them down the wrong road, and had by this means secured very many of our wagons and ambulances, before the trick was discovered, and then there were not more than half a dozen wagons intervening between the wagon carrying me and the road which led into the enemy's lines. Together with others of the wounded and wagoners the enemy were driven off and I was safely landed once again on Virginia soil, having crossed the river near Williamsport.

The next two days kept with the train and was carried to Shepardstown where I remained, being unable to report to my command, which was then engaged in battle at Boonsboro, where my friend and mess-mate, Gen. G. B. Anderson, received the wound from which he subsequently died after returning home. The regiment with Gen. D. H. Hill's command went into quarters on the Opequon, near Bunker's Hill, in ——— county, I having to be sent to Winchester on account of the serious nature of the injury to my leg, as amputation began seriously to be talked of. Here and at camp I remained until in November, and would have asked for a furlough but for the ride, &c.

I reported for duty though not recovered (and still have an indentation in the bone from the injury), when Gen. Hill relieved Col. Cristie, who had been assigned to the command of Anderson's Brigade, and put me in charge.

[Here follow notes just as they appear in the original manuscript.]

(NOTES.—Railroad at Charlestown near Harper's Ferry—Berryville, Shenandoah, Paris, Fisher's Gap, Reily, Madison C. H., Guiness Station—Dec. 1st— Dec. 3rd—Port Royal 20 miles below Fredericksburg—Dec. 13th—night of 14th placed in front line—dead horses—request not to be relieved—bunching horses—Hedge—cries of wounded—saw enemy retreating eventually—informed Gen. Hill—said mistake—freezing—Gen. Jackson coming up—sent forward to see where the enemy were—look of disappointment and chagrin—in the matter of flag—relieved of brigade command by Brig.-Gen. Ramsour—left Fredericksburg in command of 4th N. C. at peep o' day May 1st—detailed and deployed as skirmishers—Jackson—"Press Them"!—Creek—lines encountered on hill where the enemy were entrenched, and on flank May 2nd—Rodes in front attacked the enemy commanded by Siegel in person.)

The command was reorganized and perfected in drill and then assigned to destroy the Baltimore and Ohio railroad from Charlestown, the site of the execution of the notorious Kansas Ruffian, John Brown, who was executed at this point within two miles of Harper's Ferry. The work was done effectually at night by tearing up the cross-ties and putting them in large piles of twenty to thirty, and then crossing the iron rails over them and piling a few ties on top of each end of the rails, and just before day-light setting fire to them—the whole at once—the fire so warping the rails as to unfit them for use.

We were then encamped for some time near Berryville until ———— crossed the Potomac after the removal of McClellan from command, when we crossed the Shenandoah, breaking ice for the passage of the men, who had to wade one bitter cold day over the river to meet the enemy who were reported as advancing on Paris. Here, for the first time, General R. E. Rodes, one of the bravest and best officers of the Confederate army, took temporary charge of the division which subsequently became so distinguished as " Rodes Division " in the history of the Army of Northern Virginia. Here occurred a misunderstanding between Gen. Rodes and myself, which continued until the spring of 1864, and then ended by a gentlemanly and chivalrous action on the part of Gen. Rodes. The circumstances were as follows: Not knowing that Gen. Rodes was in command of the Division, and supposing that Gen. Rodes like myself was in sole command of his own brigade, came up when the troops were crossing the river, and expressing my opinion to Gen. Rodes as to the severity of the order forbidding the men to remove their pants, or shoes, which I thought ought to be done so as to enable the men to be dry after crossing, when the exercise would in a short time warm them up, Gen. Rodes said in a sharp tone he saw nothing hard in the order and that I had better go to the river and see it obeyed, that he was in command of the division, and the order emanated from him. The order was reluctantly obeyed, and after crossing the Shenandoah, as the men had necessarily straggled out of ranks, I ordered a temporary halt to enable the troops of my command to close up and recover their proper position in line. In the meantime Gen. Rodes riding to the front, upon seeing me, asked why I disregarded Gen. Jackson's order, No. —, requiring the arms to be stacked at all halts. The explanation was given and the men ordered to stack arms. Gen. Rodes then instructed me to await where I was and allow the artillery to pass him. Hour after hour passed, and no artillery came up. Finally Gen. Rodes sent a courier to know what detained. me. I sent word to him that I was waiting for the artillery. He then sent back ordering me forward. Upon reaching the small town of Paris, about two miles distant, as I approached Gen. Rodes was standing on the piazza of the hotel, and enquired in a very cross manner, " What has kept you so long?" My reply was, "Obeying your order." "What was that order?" "To let the artillery pass me." "When you saw that no artillery came up, you should have come on, as the enemy are advancing." I replied, "You had just reproved me for not obeying General Order No. —, and if you had not countermanded your order to await the arrival of the artillery, I should have remained there until Gen. Hill resumed command." He then placed himself by my side, and went on to place the command in position and said, "Halt your men here." "When I give the command 'Order arms' preparatory to stacking arms," he said, "you need not stack arms." My reply was, " It is Gen. Jackson's order, and you have just reproved me for its violation, and I shall do it." He then ordered us forward about a mile to await the advance of the enemy. We had several slight skirmishes with the enemy's cavalry, and then marched parallel with the Federal troops across the mountain at Fisher's Gap, thence down near Madison C. H. to Orange C. H., and thence down the plank road to Guiness Station, which we reached on the 1st of December, 1862, and on the 3rd were moved to Port Royal, twenty miles below Fredericksburg, where we had the first snow of any depth of the winter, and remained here protecting the river until the night of the 12th, when the enemy effected a crossing at Fredericksburg, and we were marched all night, and reached Hamilton Crossing about day, and were placed in the reserve on the extreme right of Jackson's line, and consequently the right of the Confederate forces, where we suffered considerably from the artillery of the enemy. Towards the evening of the 13th, when the first charge by the Federal troops was made, the brigade was moved forward to support the troops in the trenches, and took the front line. The cries of the wounded in the hedged old field in our front, where the enemy had charged, was heart-rending and sickening—pleading prayers to the Almighty for mercy, and begging for water to quench their thirst, which was continued all night. The expected charge of next day was deferred, and feeling anxious to meet the enemy, the officers of the command petitioned Gen. D. H. Hill to allow us to remain in the front line until the enemy did advance. Then was given us the task of burying the horses belonging to the artillery that had been killed to prevent the awful stench, not knowing how many days we would have to keep in line of battle. We found it a difficult task and not easily accomplished. During this night knew there was commotion among the enemy, and could see a light in the distance flash up and then again be darkened, and inferred that the enemy were moving to their right, and that the light was obscured as the troops passed, and flashed out at the interval between the passage of one regiment and the head of another, and sent to report the circumstance to Gen. D. H. Hill, whose reply was that I need not be uneasy, they were not going to retreat until after another effort, and be ready for their charge in the morning.

Before day next morning we were up, every man at his post, awaiting the expected charge. The fog hung low, and we waited impatiently for it to rise and show us the plain below. When I saw the enemy were not in sight, I then went forward some few hundred yards to reconnoitre, and in the meantime sent word to Gen. Hill that the enemy had disappeared from my front. Gen. Hill sent my report to Gen. Jackson, and had himself only been there a few minutes, when Gen. Jackson, accompanied by Gen. Lee, rode up to this spot, the highest eminence on that part of the field, and asked, "Who says the enemy have gone?" Gen. Hill replied, "Col.

Grimes," then turning to me, Gen. Jackson said, " How do you know ?" I replied, " I have been down as far as their picket line of the day previous, and can see nothing of them." He said, " Move your skirmish line as far as the line, and see where they are." There was a look of deep chagrin and mortification, very apparent to the observer, on the countenance of each, though nothing of the sort was expressed in words. The brigade that I then commanded was composed of the 30th, Col. Parker ; 14th, Col. Bennett ; 4th Regiment (my own) State Troops, 2nd Regiment State Troops under Col. Bynum. We then went into winter quarters, near Corbin's, and picketed the Rappahannock from Prestonburg to —— by Taylor's house. Opposite Taylor's house there were ladies, who constantly tried to signal us the movements of the enemy, particularly when Hooker moved on in April following.

During the month of February was relieved of the brigade command by Brigadier-General Ramseur. Obtained a furlough for a short time and visited home, and upon returning was occupied in drilling and disciplining the 4th Regiment, which regiment was not excelled in the army of Northern Virginia and was noted for its *esprit du corps*.

On Friday, the 1st of May, before the break of

day, we were on the march down the old Fredericksburg road towards Chancellorsville to meet Hooker's army, which had just crossed the Rapidan and striking out for Gen. Lee's rear. On this march, for the first time, Gen. Jackson appeared in full military costume, and conveyed by his personal appearance an idea of the great military hero he was. My regiment and a Mississippi command were detailed for the purpose of feeling the enemy, and were deployed to drive them in when found, my left resting on the road and acting as an extended skirmish line. Gen. Jackson rode down the turnpike with the artillery, and whenever necessary would have it to unlimber and feel the woods in our front, and would then ride along my line and upon much resistance being shown by the enemy, would say in suppressed tones, "Press them, Colonel."

In this manner, without halting, we marched down near their main body, driving them from every position, and several of their regiments leaving their knapsacks piled up where they had been thrown off when called out to oppose our onward march. Upon crossing a creek and mill-pond, driving the enemy before us, all wet, tattered and torn, and marching over the brow of the opposite hill, the whole line of the main army opened fire upon us, and if they had reserved their fire until we had gained the summit, my command would have been annihilated. As it was, they were so astounded by the suddenness of this alarming fire, that they began to fall back in confusion, when I rallied them, ordered them to "lie down," as we were protected by the eminence upon the hill above, and went forward to reconnoitre in person, when I saw that we had come upon a large force entrenched. Made a report of these facts to Gen. Jackson, and was ordered to hold my position until relieved, which was done about 12 o'clock that night, and we then went down near the turnpike to bivouac for the night. When about 8 o'clock, after noticing Generals Lee and Jackson in close conference for some time, we took up that long march for the flank movement which resulted so seriously to the Confederate cause by the loss of Gen. Jackson, though successful in an unprecedented degree in the result of the movement. After a long, tedious and circuitous route to get in the rear of Hooker's army, about 3 o'clock on Saturday evening, the 2nd of May, we were in position with Rodes' Division in front, and unexpectedly to them, fell upon Seigel's Corps that was in reserve, and drove them back for miles upon their lines behind the entrenchments, attacked them, and carried the line of earthworks, took the enemy's camp baggage, the meals, and hot coffe then boiling hot on the fire, which we found very refreshing, and just at dark when we supposed the fighting over, and was in the act of eating my supper, by an enemy's camp-fire and from his larder, then unexpectedly a brisk fire commenced, and in a few minutes cannonading, the enemy raking the woods and plank-road with grape and canister. Fearing the enemy were about to charge, I called upon my troops to occupy the breastwork which we had captured an hour previous, and be prepared for the attack.

After getting in position, and near the plank-road, I went up the road to see if I could hear anything to account for the sudden firing, when I met a party bearing a litter off the field, and enquired who it was. Some one said "Lieutenant Sumter," and upon going a step or two further I encountered Gen. Rodes, who informed me that the wounded officer was none other than Gen. Jackson, but he thought it advisable that it should be concealed from the troops for fear of disheartening them in view of the serious work ahead of us in the morning. We lay down behind the breastworks, and rested for the night.

Sunday, May 3rd, Chancellorsville. Before daybreak this morning we were called upon to hold ourselves in readiness to support other troops when called upon, as in consideration of our having borne the brunt of the fights for the two previous days, others were to take the advance. We rested just in rear of the —— Brigade, a brigade of previous good reputation, which occupied the breastworks captured by us the day previous. A staff officer rode up and directed by command of Gen. J. E. B. Stuart (who had assumed command after Gen. Jackson was wounded) the officer in command of this brigade to advance and charge the enemy, Gen. Ramseur and myself being on the plank-road and hearing the order given. This brigade commander declined to move forward his command except by order of his division commander. Gen. Ramseur then said to this staff officer, "Give me the order and I will charge." I remonstrated with him, saying as we had done the fighting of the two previous days, let this brigade move forward and we would support them. Gen. Ramseur said no, repeated his offer to advance, when this officer said, "Then you make the charge, Gen. Ramseur." Gen. Ramseur then turned to me, saying, "Let us hurry back. Call your men to attention!" which I did upon reaching the command, when he ordered the three regiments of his brigade to advance, the other regiment being detached to pretect our right. The command "Forward!" was given, and we moved up to the earthwork occupied by this brigade, and had to climb over these men now lying down behind it for protection, and over the breastworks, and again form in line of battle. Our men were entirely disgusted at their cowardly conduct, and I, myself, put my foot on the back and head of an officer of high rank in mounting the work, and through very spite, ground his face in the earth. I heard one exclaim, "You may double quick, but you will come back faster than you go." Mine, the 4th Regiment, was on the left of the command, and our left rested on the plank-road. The command was given and we advanced in a "double quick." The 4th Regiment and three companies of the 2nd Regiment never halted or fired until we had taken the enemy's works in our front and bayonetting Federal soldiers on the opposite side of the earthwork. The hill across the ravine was covered by many batteries of artillery, from forty to fifty guns, which had been scouring the woods through which we had just passed with grape and canister. Seeing their infantry driven from their works, they abandoned this artillery. The enemy made three distinct attempts to retake this work, forming their men in column by taking advantage of a ravine just beyond the turnpike, but each time were driven back with severe loss, our men acting with great courage, enthusiasm and determination.

The artillerists seeing only a small portion of the line held, now rallied again to their guns and opened upon us. About the same time my attention was called to my right and rear where I saw large numbers of the enemy fast closing up our line for retreat, (the right of Ramseur's Brigade having halted to deliver their fire upon encountering the enemy where they were engaged, while we had taken the breastwork). Seeing these Federal troops in my rear, I gave the order to abandon the captured works and fall back to the protection of the earthwork still occupied by this (———) Brigade, through whose cowardice we had suffered so severely. We crossed to the right of the plank road, and got back to our line in the best manner possible. In this charge my sword was severed by a ball, my clothes perforated in many places, and a ball embedded in my sword belt and the scabbard, and I received a very severe contusion on the foot; and upon reaching the earthwork from which we had first started, I had only sufficient strength to get over, and lost consciousness from exhaustion and pain. One of my own ambulance corps seeing my condition, came to my relief, and from a canteen was pouring water over my head when I was recalled to my senses by the voice of Gen. R. E. Rodes, our Division Commander, inquiring, "What troops are these?" The commanding officer who had refused to advance when ordered by Gen. Stuart's staff officer, said the ——— Brigade. Gen. Rodes said, "Why have you not joined in the charge?" The reply was, "We have had no orders to advance." Under the stimulus of this falsehood, I fully aroused, pronounced it a *base lie;* that I had heard the order given myself, and repeated his reply. Whereupon, Gen. Rodes took out his pistol, rode up to this officer, presented the muzzle to his head, and, with an epithet of odium, told him to forward his men, or he would blow his brains out. He then gave the command, and this (———) Brigade then moved forward, and, without firing a gun, reached the breastworks that we had taken, and found the Federal forces had evacuated the hill, and safely carried off all their artillery posted there. If these troops had moved forward in obedience to orders, and encountered the enemy, we would have advanced quickly to their support, and captured the principal part of Hooker's artillery. As it was, we met with terrific slaughter in my command, and failed to take the artillery. This closed the fighting at Chancellorsville for the infantry.

I was taken upon a litter to the hospital, where my contused foot was attended to. The next day I rode over the woods we had charged through, and examined the works we had taken, and found scores upon scores of the enemy killed, around and in front of the work, doubtless killed by my command and the three companies of the 2nd Regiment. Fortysix officers and men out of less than 300 (4th Regiment) were buried near this breastwork the next day.

This charge was as gallant, noble, and self-sacrificing as the world-renowned charge at Balaklava of the immortal "six hundred." Here Polk, my faithful servant, was tempted by the offer of $500 to sell the forage that had been procured by him for my horse, but could not be bought off.

From here we returned to near "Hamilton's Crossing," and turned in the woods to recover from our severe trials of the several previous days, and reorganized, examined, and recommended for appointment and accustom our new officers to command. Here we passed the time in drilling until about the first of June, when we took up our march for Pennsylvania. We crossed the Shenandoah near Front

Royal on the 12th of June, and attacked the enemy at Berryville.

N o t e.—Servant—Cavalry—Camp—Squirrel—Williamsport—Hagerston—Dr. McGill, &c.

REPORT OF THE FOURTH REGIMENT.

In compliance with orders, I have the honor of submitting the following report of the part taken by the 4th Regiment N. C. State Troops in the engagements around Gettysburg, Pennsylvania. On Wednesday, the 1st of July, we were encamped near Heidelburg, and were under arms and on the march by sunrise. About 4 p. m. arrived near the battlefield, and formed in line of battle, being on the left of our Brigade. After waiting a few minutes, were ordered to advance in line of battle, which was soon countermanded, and then moved by the right flank. After proceeding a few hundred yards, this Regiment, together with the 2nd Regiment, were recalled by Maj. Gen. Rodes and fronted on a hill to repel any attack from that quarter, as at that time there were indications of an advance on the part of the enemy. This position was parallel with the road down which the other two Regiments of our Brigade had moved. After a very few minutes, the enemy not advancing, and a Brigade of theirs heretofore obliquing to the left instead of advancing towards us, Gen. Rodes ordered me with the 2nd Regiment to advance. After getting from under cover of the hill, we were exposed to a severe, galling and enfilading fire from a wood to our right, which compelled me to change front towards the right. We then advanced upon the enemy, joining our Brigade, and driving them in great confusion, and but for the fatiguing and exhausting march of the day would have succeeded in capturing a very large number of prisoners. As it was, we captured more by far than the number of men in our command, but the troops were too exhausted to move rapidly, as they otherwise would have done. We were the first to enter the town of Gettysburg, and halted to rest on the road leading to Tomsfield.

We remained in that position during that night and Thursday. On Thursday evening about dark we advanced to make a night attack upon the enemy's works, but when we had approached to within a few hundred yards, and drawing the fire of their pickets, which wounded several of my men, we were recalled and placed on a road, where we remained until 3 a. m. Saturday morning, at times subjected to severe cannonading. We were then taken to the crest of hills in our rear, which position we retained until Sunday morning, when we were withdrawn. Appended is a list of casualties during this engagement. (Omitted.)

Two much cannot be said in praise of both officers and men of my command, all conducting themselves most admirably.

 I am, Major,
  Very respectfully,
   Your obedient servant,
  (Signed)   BRYAN GRIMES,
   Col. 4th N. C. State Troops.

SUMMARY OF NOTES.—Left Garysburg 20th July, 1861. Arrived at Manassas 29th July—remained until March, 1862. At Yorktown 9th April, 1862. Position outside of fortifications evacuated 3rd May, 1862. Supported other troops at Williamsburg May 5th, but not actively engaged. Seven Pines—loss 374 killed and wounded at Seven Pines. Crossed Potomac at Cheek's Ford, near Leesburg, 7th of Sept.—encamped near Frederick City, Md. Recrossed the Potomac 19th of Sept. at Sheperdstown. Remained in the Valley encamped at Bunker Hill, Winchester, Front Royal, and Strasburg. Crossed the " ridge" three times.

Chancellorsville—46 killed, 157 wounded and 58 taken prisoners out of 327 carried into action. Remained at Hamilton's Crossing until 3rd of June. On the 9th went to support of our cavalry at Brandy Station, but not engaged. Went to Valley, crossed mountains, and river at Front Royal. Assisted in driving the enemy from fortifications at Berryville and Martinsburg. Crossed the Potomac with the advance at Williamsport, Md., on 15th June, 1863. Next day advanced to Hagerstown, acting as Provost Guard of the city during the stay of the enemy in the vicinity. From there via Greencastle, Chambersburg and Shippensburg, went to Carlyle, Penn., where we went on picket duty eleven miles from Harrisburg, the capital of the State. Thence to Gettysburg via Heidelburg. Assisted in covering retreat. Recrossed the Potomac 14th July, 1863. Stopped at Darksville, then came to Front Royal, formed line of battle, resisted enemy's advance by that route. Withdrew by Luray road, crossed the mountains at Snicker's Gap, thence to Orange Court House. Sent to Morton's Ford ,to prevent the enemy crossing. On 9th Oct., 1863, ordered to Orange C. H., and went by Madison C. H. to flank the enemy near Culpepper. Enemy made formidable resistance at Warrenton Junction, and ——, which was overcome, and on the 14th the Regiment reached Bristoe's Station, tore up and destroyed railroad track, and fell back to Kelly's Ford on the Rappahannock. After remaining there several days, returned to Morton's Ford on the Rapidan river.

(Oct. 17th, 1863, Catlett's Station. We fought several hours on Wednesday, 14th inst., a running fight. * Loss from North Carolina greater than from any other State. Drove the enemy beyond Centreville. Now tearing up bridges and destroying railroads; in a few days fell back to original position. October 20th, returned home to make arrangements about withdrawing my name as candidate for Congress. November 17th, returned to the army, took command of the Brigade, Gen. Ramseur being absent.)

(Copy of letter to the Voters of the 2nd Congressional District of
North Carolina.)

Having been repeatedly solicited both through the public channels of communication as well as by private letters from numerous and influential gentlemen from the different counties composing the District, also from troops in the field, urging me to announce myself as a candidate to represent the 2nd District in our next Congress, I feel called upon, under such circumstances, to assure my friends of my proper appreciation of their kind preference, and state that if my fellow-citizens see fit to elect me, I shall esteem it a high honor to become their representative, and shall devote my entire energies earnestly to the discharge of the important duties of such a responsible position, seeking at all times, by every honorable means in the power of the Government, to restore the blessings of peace once again to our distressed land ; and my chief aim shall be to the accomplishment of that end, but fully impressed that no terms should be considered for our interest that do not recognize our complete and eternal separation from the North, and acknowledgment of our independence ; and I regret exceedingly, since allowing my name to come before the public as a candidate for their suffrages, that it is not within my power to meet my friends face to face before the election and express my views on the most momentous topics of the day, so pregnant with mighty consequences to the success of our cause ; but I will publish in a few days my opinions on these subjects, as my duties in the field will not admit of my absence from the command during the present indications of an engagement with the enemy.

    Yours very respectfully,
     (Signed)   BRYAN GRIMES.
[About October, 1863.]

(Copy of letter withdrawing from candidacy of representing 2nd Congressional District, N. C.)

To the Voters of the 2nd Congressional District of North Carolina:

Some time since, contrary to my wishes, I announced myself as a candidate to represent the 2nd Congressional District in our next Congress. Preferring to remain in active service in the field until peace and our independence is secured, and believing that I can render more effective aid in attaining that end in my present position, have under the circumstances concluded to withdraw my name, trusting that my friends will appreciate the motives which induce me to this step, assuring them that at some future time I will cheerfully assume any trust or responsibility that they may see fit to require at my hands.

Very respectfully yours,

(Signed,) BRYAN GRIMES,
Colonel 4th N. C. Troops.

(Copy of a letter to Col. Jno. A. Young, of Charlotte, who was at one time Lieutenant-Colonel of the 4th Regiment, and a member of the North Carolina Legislature when this letter was written.)

MORTON'S FORD, VA., December 6th, 1883.

My Dear Colonel: You have learned through the papers that we have been at the Yankees again, or rather it would be more proper to say that they have again taken up their "Onward to Richmond," but after a short time and a few volleys of musketry they did not move on quite so expeditiously and confidently, and upon examination of our works and defenses, concluded to "change front faced to the rear," which was done and that hurriedly, much to our chagrin, for our men had never felt more confident of victory than on that occasion. Our position was equally as strong, if not more so, than that at Fredericksburg, which you remember you considered almost impregnable. Upon the discovery that they had disappeared, our Brigade pursued with the old 4th Regiment in the lead, as usual, taking up a goodly number of stragglers—the meanest in appearance that we have ever encountered yet, being the lowest scum of the Yankee foreign population. It was really a source of congratulation and encouragement to see that they were reduced to such straits for filling their ranks. One good soldier, I know, must be equal to ten such specimens of the *genus homo*. Not one in twenty of those we captured were natives of the United States. It was reported by these prisoners that Gen. Warren's Corps was ordered to attack, but refused to do so.

I have just written a brief history of the Regiment (4th N. C. State Troops) which you can see by calling on Capt. Foote, Adjutant General, officer in charge of the "Roll of Honor." I give you leave to call for it and revise and correct it, and embellish it, if you wish it. Modesty forbids my saying near as much as I could have done in praise of it. By calling soon you can read it before Capt. Foote has transcribed it on his books. In reference to other enclosures which I have had forwarded to him, you will perceive that our loss from disease and the casualties of battle exceed five hundred. I don't know if any other Regiment can show such a record. Our Regiment is now in tolerably fair trim, but not such as it used to be.

Bye-the-bye, there has been a piece of music composed and dedicated to the Old Fourth. I sent a copy to Mrs. Grimes. Call and have her to sing it for you. I wish you to make her acquaintance. You will find her at her father's, Mr. Bryan. * *
* * * * * * * I learn that your Legislature is disposed to be fractious and intractable, like it was last winter. Can't you correct it? John, your son, is still at Richmond under the charge of the surgeons, I hope, though, not dangerously ill, but will be able to report shortly. Of

course you hear from him frequently. * * *
* * * * * * * My paper has run out, so has a legislator's patience, I fear, so good-bye.

    Truly your friend,
 (Signed,)   BRYAN GRIMES.
To Col. JOHN A. YOUNG, *Charlotte, N. C.*

[A copy of a request made of our Representatives in Congress.]

We, the undersigned, officers of the Confederate States Army from the State of North Carolina, desire to call the attention of our Representatives to the unjust and arbitrary manner of selecting general officers, and earnestly request that you call attention of the Senate to this matter before the present appointments are confirmed by that body. We believe there are instances where officers of great worth and skill, and of unexceptionable habits, and who had recommendations from general officers of high standing under whom they had served, have been overslaughed, their juniors, who were not superior to them in military skill or deportment, being appointed over them upon the recommendation of a single general officer. In some instances lieutenant-colonels, upon the recommendation of a single general officer, have been appointed over many Colonels serving in the same Brigade or Division, some of whom had received recommendations from general officers under whom they had served, and had also been mentioned in official reports for distinguished gallantry in battle. We believe this system of appointment to be unjust, and calculated to injure our cause, that it places the reputation of an officer at the mercy of his immediate superior, who, from favoritism or other impure motive, may injure his military standing by the recommendation of the appointment of a junior over him.

We would therefore suggest that resolutions to the following effect be submitted before these appointments are confirmed :

That all appointments to brigadier-generalship, now for confirmation of officers who were not entitled to expect such promotion by seniority, i. e., who were not next in rank to the vacant position ; that the number of battles in which such officer has been engaged exercising a commission at least equal to the command next below that to which he has been appointed ; also how often and by whom such officer has been recommended for promotion, and in what battles he has been complimented in official reports for distinguished conduct, be laid before the Senate for information. That the same be shown of those officers from this State amongst whose troops the vacancy is to be filled who have been passed over by such appointments. That the selection of the lower grade of general officers be not confined to the Brigade or Division in which such vacancy occurs, unless all other things are equal, then the Brigade or Division to have preference, but whenever a vacancy occurs amongst the troops of a particular State, the selection for promotion to be made from all the troops of that State serving in the army in which the vacancy occurs. We would state that the War Department has adopted a system of promotion for all grades below that of general, which we think just and efficient. That an officer cannot be promoted over his seniors unless they have been examined by a board and failed to pass their examination, or any especial act of conspicuous gallantry entitles him to such promotion. It is not sufficient to show that the officer whose promotion is asked for has behaved in battle with great skill and gallantry, but some *special act* must be stated.

Whilst we do not desire to limit the selection of general officers so much, as is necessary with the lower grades, we do desire that the appointment of juniors over seniors shall not be made without cause.

(Signed,)   E. C. BRABBLE,
Colonel 32d Regiment N. C. Troops.
J. J. IREDELL,
Major 53d Regiment N. C. Troops.
JUNIUS DANIEL,
Brigadier-General.
JAMES H. WOOD,
Lieutenant-Colonel 4th N. C. S. Troops.
WM. R. COX,
Colonel 2nd N. C. Infantry.
F. M. PARKER,
Colonel 30th N. C. Troops.
BRYAN GRIMES,
Colonel 4th N. C. State Troops.

April, 1864. Recommended for Brigadier General by Generals Daniel, Ramseur and Rodes.

(Original Copy.)
ORANGE C. H., VA., April 24th, 1864.

Gen. S. Cooper, A. & I. General:

We feel it to be our duty as North Carolina officers, and with a high sense of the good of the service, to recommend Col. Bryan Grimes, 4th N. C.

Troops, for promotion to the command of the Brigade about to be formed of the 1st, 3rd, 55th and another North Carolina Regiment. We do also recommend for this position Col. W. R. Cox, 2nd North Carolina.

Col. Grimes is among the senior Colonels from our State. He has commanded his Regiment from the battle of "Seven Pines" through all the battles in which the Army of Northern Virginia has participated, except "Sharpsburg," when he was disabled, and "1st Fredericksburg" when he commanded the Brigade of which he was senior Colonel. In the official reports of all their actions, Colonel Grimes' conduct is highly spoken of by his senior officers. In battle Colonel G. is conspicuous for skill and gallantry. He commanded for several months (from Maryland to Fredericksburg) the Brigade now commanded by Brig. Gen. Ramseur. As a disciplinarian Col. Grimes has few superiors. He is ever zealous in the performance of military duty, and in providing for and taking care of his men.

We believe the claims of Col. Grimes and Col. Cox to be very strong—by the appointment of either, the good of the service will be secured.

We, therefore, earnestly recommend their claims to his Excellency the President for promotion.

 (Signed)   S. D. RAMSEUR,.
            Brigadier-General.
 (Signed)   JUNIUS DANIEL,
            Brigadier-General.

   HEADQUARTERS RODES' DIVISION, April 27th, 1864.

I take pleasure in endorsing Col. Grimes' claims to promotion. He has served with me in this Division since its formation at Yorktown, and shown himself under all circumstances to be a good and reliable officer. He is a thorough gentleman, brave to a fault, invaluable in an action, and his habits are worthy of imitation. Respectfully forwarded.

 (Signed)   R. E. RODES,
            Major-General.

    GOLDSBORO, N. C., March 10th, 1863.

Col. Bryan Grimes entered the service as Major of the 4th North Carolina Regiment, and for more than a year had the admirable training of the lamented Gen. G. B. Anderson, who was Colonel of that Regiment.

Col. Grimes led the 4th with most distinguished gallantry at "Seven Pines," and in all the subsequent battles of the year 1862 except Sharpsburg (when he was ill). He has been in many pitched battles, and has .behaved most gallantly in them all. I think that he has seen more service than any Colonel from North Carolina. His gallantry, ripe experience, admirable training, intelligence and moral worth constitute strong claims for promotion.

(Signed)   D. H. HILL,
Major-General.

(Extracts from letters to his Wife.)

Enemy crossed at Germania Ford May 4th and 5th, 1864. Would not only take black prisoners, but no white.

May 6th.—Whipped the enemy like fury last evening. 6th. Have whipped them badly. Burnside's Corps particularly stampeded like sheep. Some of our troops did not behave so well as expected, permitting the enemy to break lines, or falling back in confusion. Gen. Lee took command in person. With waving hat in hand, charged, driving helter skelter. Our Brigade suffered slightly—charged Burnside's Corps, who broke and run before we got a good chance at them; Indians, also, who did no service.

6 o'clock Saturday morning.—Enemy are moving.

Sharp shooters feeling to see if they be in position, but hear nothing from them. Spoils immense—looks bright for Confederacy.

May 7th.—Enemy active, but nothing accomplished by them; regarded as badly whipped and demoralized. Walker Anderson killed, Col. Avery mortally wounded, Lieut. Col. Davidson prisoner, Haywood wounded.

May 9th.—Well, but greatly exhausted; was only slightly wounded in instep of left foot. Will keep on duty. Are getting the best of fights.

Battle field of Spottsylvania, May 11th.—By grace of God am still spared. The Yankees have been punished severely. We now have good breastworks, and will slay them worse than ever. Major Iredell killed yesterday; shot through the head while bravely rallying his Regiment.

May 14th.—On Thursday the enemy attacked Major-General Johnson's line, breaking through, capturing himself and Brigadier-General Stuart of Maryland, together with two thousand prisoners and twenty cannon. About 5 o'clock A. M., Ramseur's Brigade were ordered up to check the enemy, who were pressing our men, and kept them at bay for about two hours when we were ordered to charge, drove them (Ramseur's Brigade *alone*) back to the captured works, rested a few minutes, and Ramseur having been shot in his right arm and not able to keep up, and seeing no one to apply to, and seeing the necessity for speedy action, I ordered a second charge, myself leading them, and by the very boldness of the move recovered the entire works and all the guns, capturing many prisoners and killing more Yankees than the Brigade numbered men. They made repeated efforts to retake works but we successfully repulsed every attack and held possession until 4 o'clock A. M. Friday, when we were ordered to move out, which we did just before day. Gen. Lee rode down in person to thank the Brigade for its gallantry, saying, "we deserved the thanks of the country, we had saved his army." Gen. Daniel who was engaged on our left was seriously wounded and yesterday morning, at his request, I was assigned to his Brigade. He died last night. He was an excellent officer, and although I probably gained a Brigade by his death, I would have preferred to remain in *statu quo* rather than his services should be lost to the country. North Carolina has suffered seriously.

May 16th.—My escapes are regarded as miraculous when account is taken of number killed, particularly as I never order my men to perform any duty attended with danger without sharing it with them.

May 17th.—Little fighting. Yesterday enemy moved forward to move hospital with 1500 wounded which they carried to Fredericksburg. Loss to North Carolina has been very great. Many most gallant officers killed. Gen. Daniel had been recommended by Gen. Lee for Major-General.

May 18th.—Yankees charged in front but were repulsed. Considerably strengthened Grant continues to run them against us. They can't hold out much longer.

May 19th.—Enemy have disappeared ; have orders to be prepared to move so as to meet them. This is the fifteenth day since we have met them. Have been fighting more or less every day. If they would retire beyond the river and give us a breathing spell, it would be decidedly advantageous. Nearly all are fagged out and need rest.

May 20th.—We made a flank movement last evening and had a very sharp fight with the enemy. Two of the "Old Guard" killed—Gus Byees and Taylor. The old Fourth lost sixty-five killed and wounded. Daniel's Brigade behaved most gallantly, conducting itself most excellently. The bullets fell thick and heavy around me and amid it all has my life again been spared.

May 22d, Hanover Junction.—We reached here to-day after a most fatiguing jaunt. The enemy attempting to flank us as we moved down.

May 25th.—Yankees still continue obstinate and still continue to rush on to their doom, as more of them did yesterday when they came on my line. We drove them with considerable slaughter, losing but few in Daniel's Brigade, who bore the brunt of the fighting. Have now been in line of battle forty-eight hours.

May 31st.—Yesterday a hard day; the exertion I made and the fatigue undergone almost superhuman. Again this Division was called upon to make a flank movement. Whipped them but at considerable loss to Daniel's Brigade. At least three-fourths of the killed and wounded were from this Brigade. There is no doubt its being a fine body of men and will do credit to my command. Major Smith was killed and Lieutenant Lemay of Raleigh.

June 5th, 1864.—Received commission as Brigadier-General, which, according to Gen. Rodes' request, bore date of 19th of May, 1864, on which occasion on a flank movement near Fredericksburg, towards the rear of Grant's army, I handled the

Brigade with such efficiency that Gen. Rodes approached me soon after the battle, and shaking me by the hand, said: "You have saved Ewell's Corps, and shall be promoted, and your commission shall bear date from this day." After remaining in position sufficiently long for the wounded and stragglers to come up, retired to position of the Corps in the morning. My rank is permanent, so direct your letters hereafter to Brig.-Gen. Grimes.

June 7th.—Another flank movement last evening; did not amount to much. Last night came to this spot near Richmond, and for the first time in thirty odd days have come in the woods to encamp, massed by regiments. Have heretofore rested on our arms in line of battle.

June 8th.—Had orders to be prepared to move at daylight, but are still here near Cold Harbor. My old Regiment made application to be transferred to this Brigade, which I hope will be granted. I have an affection for them, having been associated with them so long.

June 13th, near Southana River.—Marched over thirty miles to-day over sandy road. Everything and everybody exhausted. Left Cold Harbor at 2 o'clock A. M. Appears as if we are going to the Valley of Virginia. Are now on the Charlottesville road. Must either be after Hunter or going into Maryland. I pray Christ that it will end more successfully than the other invasion.

June 15th, near Gordonsville.—Stopped here to camp for night. Think we will move up the Valley.

June 18th.—In the morning we take the cars for Lynchburg, after a most fatiguing and oppressive march. During Gen. Rodes' absence to visit his wife, I have command of the Division.

June 21st, 1864, Top of Blue Ridge.—Have been pursuing Yankees at such a rapid gait, haven't had time to write. Been almost without rations—hard marching, and nothing to eat. Start before day, not stop till dark, except to rest for ten minutes. We move immediately.

' June 22nd, Salem, Va.—Since leaving Richmond have scarcely rested any to invigorate our exhausted energies, and with it all a deficiency of rations. For the duration of forty-eight hours my Brigade did not have a mouthful of bread, and but little flesh—very little straggling and very little complaining. Occasionally, when Gen. Rodes or Early passed the line, the cry was, "Bread, bread, bread;" but through it all, we made a forced march for the last day, and arrived too late to inflict much damage on the enemy, which was very annoying, as we expected to get supplies from them, but instead found only empty wagons and worthless provisions. At Lynchburg the ladies sent us supplies of good edibles for the General officers. At Liberty I was invited out to breakfast, which I enjoyed very much.

NOTE.—July, 1864, I returned home on sick furlough, being so completely worn out from fatigue and hardship as to bring on a severe attack. Was in hospital in Lynchburg a few days before leaving for Raleigh. Was quite unwell when I returned, and had surgeon's certificate of unfitness for duty, but imagined that duty called me back to the army.

Staunton, August 6th.—Arrived here sooner than I expected. Found Polk and my horse Warren, who had been sent home to be taken care of, waiting for me. Shall leave early in the morning for Winchester. Learn that our troops moved into Maryland Thursday.

New Market, August 8th.—Have stopped for dinner. I have found a very agreeable travelling companion in Captain Burrill, a first cousin of General Lee. Without his company this horseback ride of one hundred miles would have been very lonely.

August 10th, Nort Fork of Shenandoah River.—Have learned that our troops have returned, and are encamped at Bunker Hill, where I will rejoin them to-night.

Stevenson's Depot, August 12th.—My surmises that they would not remain long at Bunker Hill are correct, and the indications are that we will not stay here long, but cannot conjecture in what direction we will move. General Early out-generals all of us. No one can guess when he is going to move, or where he will next bring up. The Yankees begin to think him ubiquitous.

Strasburg, Aug. 13th.—Have been expecting a fight ever since I rejoined my command last Wednesday, but have had none as yet. We have through strategic movements fallen back from Bunker Hill to this place. Have been sick, but am better. Have felt so badly, I regretted having gone contrary to advice in returning so soon.

August 14th.—The enemy are very quiet to-day. This morning we drew up to attack them, but they fell back, and we quietly returned to our rest in the woods.

Strasburg, Aug. 15th.—Another day of rest and free from fighting. Had a delightful serenade from my old command.

Strasburg, Aug. 16th.—Another quiet day, and from indications think it may be several weeks before we have an engagement; for the enemy, as well as ourselves, are erecting breastworks. General Anderson will join us, when, as we will be tolerably strong, we may strike a blow at them.

August 18th, Near Winchester.—Again have we driven the enemy from position, and followed them to this place, they still falling back, and not showing much fight. Their numbers are double ours. We were joined by Gen. Anderson's force this morning; also a Division of Cavalry. Could not write yesterday, was on the march all day. Now 2 o'clock, and have not broken my fast. Am invited out to dinner, which I accept with pleasure.

Bunker Hill, Aug. 19th.—The enemy continue to fall back, and we have pressed until reaching the present position. What is Gen. Early's intention I can't say.

Bunker Hill, Aug. 20th.—We have an admirable camp, but have had nothing but beef and flour, not even hog meat or salt, to help along. We remain here a day or two to threaten the enemy. I received orders this morning, when it was thought the enemy were advancing, to make a big show of fight and bluff them off, if possible; but if they came in force, to hold them a little while, to give the others time to retreat, and then fall back.

Charlestown, Va., August 21st.—I have had to-day a good many killed and wounded, we being in advance, but have not had all my command engaged. The enemy have a large force between us and Harper's Ferry, which Early is demonstrating upon, and are contesting the ground most stubbornly. This is a mere feint to frighten them and cover some important move on our part. I have no idea we will fight here, for the enemy outnumber us three to one, and Early knows two well the importance of preserving his army.

Charlestown, August 22d.—My experience to-day has been varied. Early this morning we pitched into the Yankees and drove them through Charlestown to their position on Boliver heights where they are watching us and occasionally throwing a shell at us. I have command of the front line, and this morning while visiting the picket line as soon as they spied us their artillery opened upon us, which passed within a few feet of my horse.

August 23rd, near Harper's Ferry.—Amid the fighting have escaped injury so far. Find everything more plentiful here than in any part of the valley, and the people anxious to conduce to our pleasure by every means in their power. They are loyal to the backbone.

Charlestown, August 24th.—Another day spent between Charlestown and Harper's Ferry, the enemy occasionally demonstrating, and about 12 o'clock to-day their cavalry charged our picket line and drove them in, and for the first time in many a day I doubled quicked to reach my command in time to form line of battle, so as to give them a fitting reception. At the time I was visiting a neighboring Brigade, but reached my own and formed line of battle before any other troops. After remaining in line half an hour found there was no use and returned to our resting place.

August 27th, Leestown, near Shepardstown, Va. Have been so busy for two days have not had time to write. Wednesday we left Charlestown and advanced towards Shepardstown. When about half way the enemy's cavalry attacked Breckinridge's command, which caused a halt, when Rodes' Division came up, my Brigade being in advance, we formed line of battle, threw out one Regiment as skirmishers, and advanced upon them, driving them before us. We chased them for upwards of two hours, many of the men fainting from exhaustion. We drove them entirely from the Baltimore and

Ohio Railroad and beyond the turnpike, when we halted to rest and found ourselves two miles in advance of any other troops, when at the beginning we were the third Division in the line. And again that morning, when near Shepardstown, and the others had halted for our approach, we came upon the enemy and followed them until they crossed the Potomac. Whenever we are able to get them in a run, I feel really like a boy and enjoy the sport immensely. After halting, as we supposed for the night, and I had engaged supper for self and staff, we received orders to move on the Martinsburg pike, but I could not leave without that supper, as I had eaten nothing since sunrise that morning. About 10 o'clock that night reached the ground allotted to us, and after placing men in position, laid down and slept as quietly as an infant.

Bunker's Hill, August 29th.—Am well.

August 30th.—Still at Bunker's Hill quiet.

August 31st.—Severe march and skirmishing.

September 1st, 1864.—At 8 A. M. we were called out and moved down the road a few miles when we encountered the Yankee cavalry and pushed on, driving them through Martinsburg, leaving large quantities of pork, corn, oats, clothes, shoes, boots, &c. I enjoyed the sport, and after driving them ten miles beyond Martinsburg, came back to camp without the loss of a single man, and few wounded. We inflicted a right severe punishment upon the enemy, besides a big fright. They thought we were on the route to Williamsport, Md. My Brigade was the only one which went beyond the town, the others being halted on the edge of town.

Camp near Winchester, September 4th.—We are having quite a stirring time, and giving the Yankees a hot time, and doing a great deal of marching ourselves.

September 6th, 1864, Stevenson's Depot.—We have moved down in the direction of Berryville, where we formed to attack the enemy, but found them so strongly entrenched after skirmishing for a couple of hours we retired for the night, when we reached camp wet, and exhausted, and hungry, without a wagon or tent to shelter us from the rain, spent the night all exposed and woke up next morning drenched to the skin. About ten o'clock began to retire from the front of the enemy, and moved down toward this point, where we started from the day before. When within a couple of miles learned that the enemy was between us and our encampment, and driving our cavalry before them. My Brigade being in advance formed and prepared to fight. Charged them at double quick, and had a most exciting chase, breaking them in every effort they made to make a stand and drove them until night came on and prevented further pursuit. This fight was during one of the severest rains that I have ever seen fall. Tom Devereux had his horse killed under him, and kept up with me on foot until I ordered him to stop. Both he and Tuck Badger behave remarkably well under fire.

September 7th, '64, Stevenson's Depot.—Weather terrible. No orders to move to-day.

September 10th, 1864, Stevenson's Depot.—The weather continues very rainy. We are now very much in need of clothes and shoes, there being at least two hundred barefooted and half naked men in my command. Am using every exertion to get them clothed, but with all our rags and nakedness can put up a most beautiful fight. The men go into action with spirit, and I feel like a boy after being in a fight a few minutes. To-morrow we break up camp and again go to Bunker Hill. Gen. Early has been very successful in all his manoeuvres.

September 11th, 1864, Bunker Hill.—We have. again changed. Are now nearer the Potomac than on yesterday. Expect to move again to-day. Had to drive the enemy from this point so we could take possession. I learn that the enemy's loss was very heavy Monday when my Brigade charged them.

Stevenson's Depot, September 13th, 1864.—We are under marching orders. From the report of artillery it will be up the Valley, as the enemy appears to be advancing in that direction. The nights are very cold, find two or three blankets comfortable.

Stevenson's Depot, September 16th and 17th.— Had a serenade last night given by the band of the "Old Fourth Regiment," which I appreciate as a mark of respect and esteem from my old command. Anderson's Division returned to Richmond. Only our original force left.

Strasburg, September 20th, 1864.—Yesterday we had a most terrible fight at Winchester, and we were very roughly handled by the enemy. We lost a great many men, and our troops did not behave with their usual valor. With great exertion on my part and that of my staff mine did better than any other, but that was not as well as I desired. Gen. Rodes was killed. Capt. London, Capt. Still and Lieut. Barnes, of my staff, were wounded. The horse of one of my couriers and my own horse killed under me, and for nine hours was under heavy fire, and men falling around me almost every instant. Have been as near exhausted as a man could well be, not slept ten hours in forty-eight. It was the most trying day of the war to me, when after what I supposed was a victory, I saw the enemy break over our cavalry and dash in rear of our troops and cut and hack away at them. Am truly thankful for my safety.

Strasburg, September 22d.—Requested Lieut. Barnes to telegraph you for fear the report current in the rear of my being killed might reach you. It was a most terrible day. In the beginning we drove the enemy and killed many, and could have driven them into Harper's Ferry but for the troops on our left. Our cavalry first gave way, our infantry were flanked, then there was a general fall back. Ramseur has been assigned to this Division and Pegram to Ramseur's old command. Gen. Rodes' place cannot be supplied. He is a serious loss to the Confederacy. Capts. London, Still and Lieut. Barnes are a great loss to me; their aid was invaluable. Lieut. Howard was mortally wounded and fell into the hands of the enemy.

New Market, September 24th.—Have been so busy no time to write. Am well and safe after most fatiguing and dangerous fighting for five days. My escapes have been miraculous.

Camp near Port Republic, September 25th.—We

have reached a place of safety, after one of the most harassing weeks of anxiety ever spent by me, less on my own account than that of others. It has been fight all day and retreat all night. Am completely exhausted.

Near Port Republic, Sept. 26th.—A week this morning since we left camp on September 19th at Stevenson's Depot, when, in less than one hour, encountered the enemy, and, forming line, attacked him; drove some distance, inflicting most terrible punishment upon him, and then halted.

Everything up to 4 o'clock in the afternoon looked bright, and promised well for a complete victory. The enemy had turned their wagons back to Harper's Ferry about 4 o'clock, then their Cavalry charged our Cavalry, which was on the left of our Infantry, which gave way in confusion, and their forces came down on the left and rear of our column, when the troops began to give way in that quarter. About which time I received orders to swing back and front them from that direction, allowing the right of my Brigade to remain stationary. Upon coming into the open field, I perceived everything to be in the most inextricable confusion—horses dashing over the field, cannon being run to the rear at the top of the horses' speed, men leaving their command, and scattering in confusion. My men seeing this state of things began also to show symptoms of alarm, which I in a great measure checked, threatening to blow the brains out of the first man who left ranks, and succeeded in quieting them down and keeping them under control. Then directed my attention to arresting the flight of others, and many a fellow felt the full weight of my best blows from my sword. During this time the Yankee Cavalry was dashing among them, cutting and hewing right and left. We then attempted to fall back slowly, confronting them and fighting every inch of the ground which was done through to Winchester and some four miles south of that point. The ladies of Winchester came out in the streets when the stampede first began and formed across the streets and entreated the stragglers to return, but without success. I have already told you about having my horse killed under me, and my escapes from death on that day appeared marvelous, for from ten o'clock in the morning until after eight at night, I was in the thickest of the fight. Capt. London, poor fellow, was shot, and caught by me as he fell. Capt. Foster the same day was killed. That night we marched until about 2 o'clock when we lay down and slept until about 4, at which time we were again on the road and reached Strasburg about 12 M. on Tuesday, cooked up rations, and slept off our fatigue of the previous twenty-four hours. I have never exerted myself so much in my life and my voice was completely gone; could scarcely speak above a whisper. I was as sore as a boil all over, and had to have Polk (his body servant) to rub me over with liniment. On Wednesday we erected breastworks, and prepared for the advance of the enemy, and felt very secure of holding the position of the command in front. Were busily engaged day and night up to about one o'clock Thursday the 22d, when they attacked our skirmishers and drove them in; did not attack the line of battle. About 3 o'clock we perceived two columns moving up the side of the mountain to our left, when the cavalry was again fronted. I then urged upon Ramseur, who commanded our Division, to send a Brigade or two over to their assistance, knowing that the cavalry would run if attacked, but he declined to do so until he could communicate with Gen. Early, and then sent Cox's Brigade, but alas! it was too late. During that hour I suffered more than I've ever done in my life. My anxiety for the fate of the army was intolerable. I deployed three of my regiments to protect my flank in case of an attack, which about 4 o'clock came like an avalanche. The cavalry breaking, my skirmish line presented but a feeble resistance. The enemy attacked me on my left flank, front and rear at the same time. I remained, fought until Ramseur came up and told me to save my Brigade if possible. The colors of the United States troops were then in less than a hundred yards of me. I moved off by my right flank, firing to the front and left as I marched. Thinking that we were going to fight in the trenches, had sent my horse to a hollow for protection. A while before this time I had fallen in walking down the trenches and sprained my ankle, and was unable to hobble along but very slowly. Through mistake my horse had been carried from the place that I had ordered him, and I found myself afoot when I ordered the troops to leave. As we marched by the flank we were firing to the right, left and rear. Upon attempting to put my men in position in line, I found it almost an impossibility, on account of the nearness of the enemy, and that I would be left behind to fall into the hands of the Yankees. Just then a cannon ball cut down two horses in a caisson, and the drivers were engaged in getting the others loose from their harness. Two were loosened and the drivers had mounted them before I could get up, and others were cutting out the other two. To procure one of these horses was a matter of life and death with me, and while one of these artillerymen was cutting away, I vaulted into the saddle and told him to hurry up, that I must have that horse. He didn't take time to parley with me, but ran off, leaving the horse still fastened by one trace to the horse that had been killed, and I out with my knife and began to cut away, when another driver who had by this time disentangled his horse, loosened this trace for me, and I put spurs to my horse, and the Yankees then not over fifty yards from me, and I had an open field of two hundred yards to run the gauntlet through, and but few other objects in view for them to shoot at. My escape was almost miraculous. On my way I found Col. Winston broken down and took him behind me. Overtook my troops and formed into line, made several short stands, but the troops on all sides were too much demoralized to make a successful fight, and it was fall back all the time, and I was carried along in the current only by order when I found no support. This state of thing continued up to nine o'clock that night, when we finally checked the enemy, and travelled all night long until we reached Mt. Jackson, where rested several hours forming line of battle, and then kept the enemy in check until dark, when we continued our retreat to Rudes' Hill, near New Market, and about 9 o'clock next morning the enemy again began to press. We remained until 12 o'clock, when we found that they were flanking us in the same manner that they had done on the two previous occasions, and Gen. Early then began to withdraw us in line of battle, which was very successfully done until about night, when we withdrew to Brown's Gap and Port Republic, the place of one of Jackson's great victories. Here we were called upon next day to go out and drive off their cavalry, which we did, inflicting considerable loss upon them.

Weir's Cave, September 28th.—Moved around a good deal yesterday, but halted for the night near where we started in the morning, except we were on the north side of the Shenandoah. Reported the enemy are falling back to the Potomac.

Waynesboro, September 29th.—Yesterday had a most disagreeable march, not arriving in camp until four o'clock this morning, travelling all night in the rear of a wagon train to protect it from Yankee cavalry, who were threatening on all sides. Troops beginning to recover from effects of last week's misfortunes; in tolerable fighting trim, and anxious to retrieve their lost reputation.

Waynesboro, October 1st, 1864.—Yesterday was a day of rest very essential to our comfort, for our energies were about exhausted. The enemy are reported to be falling back down the Valley, which I hope is so, unless we had an opportunity of thrashing him.

Mount Sydney, October 2nd.—Nothing of interest.

Mount Sydney, October 3rd.—The enemy slowly retiring and we following him up, but Early will profit by past experience and not risk too much.

Mount Sydney, October 4th, 1864.—Another day of rest and what was quite as much needed, a good dinner. The gentleman with whom we dined was ransomed by his wife and daughters paying all their jewelry and silver, and the house redeemed by payment of $40 in gold. Enemy near Harrisburg few miles from here.

Mount Sydney, October 6th.—This is our fourth day of rest, and have made use of it to recruit my exhausted energies. Have been drilling my men, for I know the necessity of drilling and discipline to make good soldiers, as I am anxious that those under my command should be.

Harrisonburg, October 7th.—Again on the march following the enemy.

Camp near New Market, October 9th.—It is probable we will remain in our present position for some time. Enemy been driven below Strasburg, and as they destroyed everything on their retreat, we have not the wherewithal to subsist our army on. Country a perfect desolation. All stock and provisions destroyed.

New Market, October 10th.—Ordered down the turnpike to meet the enemy. Having gone four miles, were ordered to return to camp.

New Market, October 11th.—Just received orders to cook two days' rations and be ready to move at sunrise in the morning.

Near Woodstock, October 13th.—Are moving towards Strasburg. Enemy reported as lower down the Valley.

Near Strasburg, October 14th.—Yesterday afternoon attacked the enemy, gained quite a little victory.

Near Strasburg, Oct. 15th.—Stationary. Nothing of importance.

Near Strasburg, Oct. 16th.—Enemy quiet on other side Cedar Creek.

Near Strasburg, Oct. 17th.—Yesterday reported to

Gen. Rosser (Cavalry General). About dark mounted my men behind his, took a by-path over the mountains, over the most rugged roads I ever travelled. About 3 o'clock came up in rear of Yankee camp. Dismounting my men, prepared to charge them. We had been informed a Cavalry Division were encamped at this place, but found only forty men, every one of whom we captured with their horses. Had a pleasant time.

Near Strasburg, Oct. 18th.—Enemy remarkably quiet.

New Market, Oct. 20th.—Yesterday morning, after marching all night, flanked the enemy in their position, whipping them badly, and driving them from their breastworks, capturing twenty-odd pieces of artillery, driving them several miles. Our left wing shamefully gave way, which necessitated the drawing in of our lines, which was done in considerable confusion. At that time the Yankee Cavalry charged and completely routed our men. It was impossible to check the flight, officers and men behaving shamefully. Twice the Yankees got between me and the route I had to travel, which rendered it necessary for me to take the woods to avoid capture. About seven o'clock arrived at a place on Fisher's Hill, where we halted to endeavor to gather up the stragglers and rearrange our troops. After resting a few hours, fell back to this place. It was the hardest day's work I ever engaged in—trying to rally the men. Took our flags at different times, begging, commanding, entreating the men to rally—would ride up and down the lines, beseeching them by all they held sacred and dear, to stop and fight, but without any success. I don't mean my Brigade only, but *all*. The demoralization was too great. All my exertions were of no avail. I was riding a horse that I captured in our night attack upon the cavalry which I mention in my letter of last Monday, and had him killed by a shell early in the engagement, while on his back, the shell not missing my leg two inches. Afterwards found a horse on the field, rode him the remainder of the day. He also was struck, but not much hurt. Had a ball to strike me on the leg, but so slightly that the blow was scarcely perceptible, the ball having expended its force. General Ramseur was wounded mortally, and fell into the hands of the enemy. General Battle, of Alabama, severely wounded. The only salvation for this army and the country will be to inflict severe punishment on all who fail to discharge their duty. There will be a general Court Martial this afternoon, and all delinquents will be tried.

Camp near New Market, Oct. 22d.—I am now in command of Rodes' old Division—very busily engaged all my time in correcting abuses that have crept into the department during the long and arduous campaign—inspecting camp, attending drills, and hope if we are allowed a few weeks to discipline these troops, to have them as good and efficient as they were in their best days.

New Market, Oct. 23rd, 24th and 25th.—Still quiet. Busily engaged re-organizing.

October 26th.—Enemy quiet for the present. Don't know how long it will last. Have no idea when we will go into winter quarters.

New Market, Oct. 27th to 31st.—Employed in drilling and disciplining troops. All have the greatest confidence in General Early. No blame can be attached to him for our failures. Simply want of discipline among the troops.

(Report of the part taken by Rodes' Division in the action of October 19th, 1864.

HEADQUARTERS RODES' DIVISION, October 31st, 1864.

Capt. SAM'L J. C. MOORE, *A. A. G.:*

CAPTAIN: In obedience to orders from Corps Headquarters, I have the honor of submitting the following report as the part taken by Rodes' Division in the action on the 19th October, 1864:

About dark on the evening of the 18th the Division moved from camps on Fisher's Hill and was halted for an hour or more near the pike, in order that Maj.-Gen. Gordon in command of the force, who was to move to the enemy's rear, could communicate with Lieut.-Gen. Early.

This halt was caused, as I unofficially learned, in consequence of information received that the enemy were fortifying that evening on their left flank. About 8 P. M. the march was resumed and after passing the stone bridge filed to the right and passed by a circuitous route around the base of Fort Mountain, by a blind path, where the troops had to march in single file. The order of March was Gordon, Rodes, Pegram. Upon reaching the Shenandoah, where crossed by the Manassas Gap Railroad, the column was halted and massed for the rear to close up. So soon as this was done, about 1 A. M., we again moved forward, following the track of the railroad until near Bucktown Station, where we again halted for an hour and a half waiting the arrival of the cavalry, who crossed the river in advance and drove in the enemy's pickets.

About four and half A. M. the infantry commenced crossing the Shenandoah near Col. Bowman's house in two columns. The passage was effected with great rapidity and in good order though the rear necessarily had to doublequick for some distance to close up. The order of march was as follows : Battle, Cook, Cox, Grimes. On arriving within a half a mile of the Valley Pike, Battle's Brigade was formed parallel with the same, and moved forward in line of battle. The other Brigades continued moving by the flank for about three hundred yards, when they were faced to the left and ordered forward changing direction to the right. Battle soon struck the Eighth Corps of the enemy, and charging, gallantly drove them in great confusion but was himself seriously wounded whilst nobly leading his Brigade, the command of which then devolved on Lieut.-Col. Robeson, 5th Alabama. Cook and Cox continued to advance, swinging to the right, driving the enemy in their front with but slight resistance for upward of half a mile, when Gen. Cox reporting that he was flanked on the left, a temporary halt was made until reinforcements were sent forward, when these two Brigades again advanced, Cook capturing several cannon, caissons, ammunition, wagons, &c.

This movement left a wide interval between

Cook's right and Battle's left, which was subsequently filled by Pegram's Division. In the meantime Grimes' Brigade was recalled from the left and moved by the right flank through the abandoned camp of the Eighth Corps, which had been completely routed, faced to the front, and advanced to the pike, connecting with Battle's right. This formation was perfected about sunrise.

The enemy being then in position on a small creek to the left of the Pike, with their artillery on a high ridge in their rear, and firing into our line of battle, but the smoke and fog obscured the troops so that their fire was inaccurate. Here Major-Gen. Ramseur had skirmishers thrown to the front and to the right driving the sharpshooters of the enemy from Middletown. The Division remained here perhaps half an hour, until a battery was brought into position on the right of the Pike, when Gen. Ramseur again ordered an advance, which was made in good order, and with a gallantry never exceeded. In this advance Battle's Brigade charged a battery in its front, capturing in addition to six guns many prisoners and a flag. The Sixth Corps was found posted on a hill in rear of this battery, and made a most stubborn resistance. Grimes' Brigade was ordered forward and charged them most gallantly, but being greatly overlapped on both flanks was forced to fall back and reform after advancing as far as the cemetery. At this time there was an interval of three hundred yards between this and Battle's Brigade. Colonel Smith's Brigade of Wharton's Division was now brought into action on Grimes' right and charged the same wooded hill, but was likewise repulsed, when Wofford's Brigade of Kershaw's Division, which had been ordered to report to Major-Gen. Ramseur, arrived on the ground and was posted behind a stone fence to the right of Grimes, it not being thought advisable to move against the strong position of the enemy.

The artillery was at this time, about 8 A. M., massed on the hills near the Pike and the infantry remained quiet until by a concentrated fire from the artillery the Sixth Corps was dislodged from its position, where they had erected temporary breastworks of rails, stones, &c. Upon this hill the Division was reformed, cartridge boxes refilled and rested upwards of an hour. During this time skirmishers were advanced and found that the enemy had again made a stand at the edge of the woods, about three fourths of a mile in advance. We then moved forward and joined our left to Kershaw's right, halting in the road leading from Middletown and at right angles to the Pike. Here again we halted perhaps for an hour, and then moved forward in echelon by Brigade from the left, which was occupied by Cook with Cox's Brigade in reserve, and took position behind a stone fence. During this time the enemy were firing from their artillery, engaging ours on the hills in our rear. Our skirmishers all the while were engaged with those of the enemy and who had driven in our left, but they in turn were repulsed by our line of battle. In this position Grimes' Brigade was about one hundred yards to the right and rear of Battle's with an interval of from two to three hundred yards between his right and Pegram's left. At half past three P. M. our skirmishers were driven in and the enemy advanced their line of battle. Grimes' Brigade was "doublequicked" upon the line with Battle to meet this advance on the part of the enemy, and Cox moved up on a line with Cook and to his left, which advance was repulsed most gallantly, the enemy fleeing in disorder and confusion, throwing down their arms and battle flags in their retreat. The musketry on our left still continued to increase and at the time our troops were cheering for this repulse of the enemy, the line on our left was seen to give back, and the troops to retreat without any organization. Gen. Ramseur then ordered the different Brigades of this Division to fall back and form on a stone fence about two hundred yards in rear, which was promptly done, and the advance of the enemy in our front prevented. While holding this position, the gallant and chivalrous Gen. Ramseur was mortally wounded and brought from the field. The troops on the left had by this time entirely given way, and were running to the rear in great confusion. The enemy were then in front and to the left and rear of the left flank of this Division, when they began to fall back in the same disorderly manner as those on the left.

Our organization up to this time was intact. Upon the order being given to retire, did so, but the stampede on left was caught up, and no threats or entreaties could arrest their flight. Great and repeated exertions were made by the officers of the higher ranks to check the men, but all their exertions were unavailing.

Upon reaching the south side of Cedar Creek, a few, perhaps to the number of two hundred, from Cook's and Grimes' Brigades, formed on the right of the Pike near Hupp Hill, but when the stream of stragglers came running over the hill, with the cry that the cavalry were across the creek, and prepared to charge, these few likewise scattered, and could not be kept together. Up to the hour of 4 P. M., the troops of this Division, both officers and men, with a few exceptions, behaved most admirably, and were kept well in hand, but little plundering, and only a few shirking their duty. After that hour, all was confusion and disorder. The Brigade commanders conducted themselves, each and all, with great coolness and judgment, and are deserving of especial mention, using all possible efforts to check their troops, but without success.

The death of the brave and heroic soldier, General Ramseur, is not only a loss to this Division, but to his State and the country at large. No truer or nobler spirit has been sacrificed in this unjust and unholy war.

The conduct of the officers composing the staff of this Division cannot be too highly lauded for their gallantry and efficiency: Major Peyton for the coolness and promptness with which he conveyed orders on the field; Major Hutchinson for his efficiency, who was captured, escaped from the enemy, and again captured late in the evening; Captain Randolph displayed his usual daring; Major Whiting, Inspector, rendered signal services by preventing all straggling and plundering; and Lieut. Richmond, A. D. C., for his assistance and alacrity in transmitting orders.

For the conduct of others who deserve especial mention, you are respectfully referred to reports of Brigade commanders herewith transmitted.

I am, Captain,
Very respectfully,
Your obedient servant,
(Signed) BRYAN GRIMES,
Brig. Gen. Command'g Division.

(Further Extracts from Letters to his Wife.)

Near New Market, November 1st, 1864.—The duties of camp are suspended to-day for the purpose of commemorating our respect and attachment for our two late commanders, Rodes and Ramseur. I could not participate in the meeting, owing to a summons from General Early to meet all Division Commanders, which detained me six hours.

Camp near New Market, November 2d to 4th.— I am still here. It has rained incessantly for two days. Am busy re-organizing Rodes' Division, which I still command.

New Market, November 5th.—No news from the enemy. They are still near Strasburg. Our movements depend on theirs. If they reinforce Grant, we will demonstrate in order to draw them back.

Headquarters Rodes' Division, November 6th.—Yesterday moved camp to present position, where we have abundance of wood and water. The mountains are covered with snow this morning—very hard on barefooted and half naked men.

November 7th.—Weather continues bad.

November 8th and 9th.—Still at New Market. Yesterday at Early's Headquarters learned the enemy had 36,000 effective men for the field. More than three times our number. At recent fights they must have had at least five to one. If not for their cavalry, we could soon drive their infantry out of the Valley. When the history of the war is written, and the disparity of the forces engaged is considered, we will come out with honor; and if justice is done, it will be shown that we have done our duty.

Learned that after election in the United States, that their troops would be moved to some other quarter. They are still fortifying Winchester.

Camp near New Market, November 10th.—We leave here to-day to demonstrate against the enemy, to cause to return with their troops to prevent reinforcement of Grant. If we accomplish that, it will be all that can be expected of us.

November 12th.—Have again advanced, and are between Middletown and Winchester. Enemy falling back—don't seem disposed to fight.

November 13th.—We found the enemy, and General Early having accomplished his purpose, retired last night, and are on our way to our old camp.

November 14th.—Have just reached our old camp. Too tired to write. In five days have been eating both meals at night—one before day in the morning, the other after dark.

November 15th to 19th.—Still at New Market. Weather bitterly cold.

November 20th to 22d.—Weather still continues bad, but with a good chimney to my tent keep tolerably comfortable. General Early does not speak of going into winter quarters.

Headquarters Rodes' Division, near New Market, November 23d.—Yesterday morning just before day Gen. Early sent me word that the enemy were advancing and to take my command out to meet them. The ground was covered with snow but in half an hour we were under arms and on the way to meet them. After going about seven miles down the turnpike to Rudes' Hill found that our cavalry had been driven through Mount Jackson and the enemy had crossed the north fork of the Shenandoah and were advancing rapidly. I rode forward, reconnoitered, put my men in position and attacked them. There were about 4000 of them, all cavalry. When we struck them they made a bold stand and attempted to charge, but we pressed the shot into them so steadily and rapidly that they could not stand it, and began to retreat in disorder, which I pressed all the harder, and drove them five miles, routing them every time they attempted to make a stand. My men were pretty well used up with fatigue when I discontinued the pursuit and returned to camp cold, hungry, and broken down after my men had marched and waded twenty-four miles.

Headquarters Rodes' Division, November 24th and 28th.—We are here with the thermometer down to about 20 deg. and the coldest nights imaginable. Hope we will go into winter quarters soon.

Headquarters Rodes' Division.—Yesterday had a long ride and returned after dark, but feel that I will here accomplish a good thing if the Yankee cavalry venture another reconnoissance to find out where we are. Our object is to get in their rear and cut off all * * * and as there will be but one ford to the river by which they can rejoin their command, and all arrangements are made to get possession of that ford by taking a circuitous route with our Division while the others demonstrate in front. But if they don't advance in ten days, we will miss an opportunity to inflict a severe blow upon their cavalry. Provisions and forage are very scarce. Some of our troops have had unground corn issued to them.

Headquarters Rodes' Division, November 30th.—Everything quiet with only a rumor that Gen. Rosser had whipped the enemy at Moorefield. When he returns, it is thought we will go into winter quarters.

Headquarters Rodes' Division, December 2d.—Gen. Rosser's success was quite brilliant, destroying two bridges, two hundred wagons, nine locomotive engines, besides immense amount of quartermaster's and commissary stores, and capturing nine pieces of artillery, 500 prisoners, 1000 horses and mules, and several hundred beef cattle. This is the expedition I wrote you about in former letter.

Headquarters Rodes' Division, near New Market, December 2d.—I think it probable that we will reach the point at which we are to winter about the 10th of this month.

December 4th.—Still at New Market.

December 6th.—We are again disappointed in receiving no orders to prepare for winter quarters.

All manner of conjectures are rife. I think Gen. Early is actuated simply and solely by what he considers the good of the service, and is awaiting definite information as to the intention of the enemy, and contrary as it would be to my wishes, if we could accomplish any commensurate good, would be willing again to go down the Valley and attack Sheridan, and if necessary stay there, although it would interfere with my long cherished desire to spend a quiet winter, but in my present position the public interest is to be considered before private preference, and the higher a man rises in the military service the fewer privileges can he enjoy, for he cannot ask indulgence when he feels the good of the country will be jeopardized, and as I am now commanding a Division, will have to remain here until some one else comes to fill the place.

Near New Market, December 8th.—Two of our Divisions, Gordon's and Pegram's, left yesterday. I presume some important move is on hand. The enemy have sent one of their Corps from our front.

Headquarters Rodes' Division, December 10th.—This morning the whole surface of the earth is covered with snow two inches deep.

Near New Market, December 13th.—Have orders to proceed to Richmond to-morrow morning—expect to reach there Friday or Saturday.

Richmond, December 16th.—Arrived here early this morning, and am awaiting orders from Gen. Lee.

Headquarters Rodes' Division, near Petersburg, Dec. 18th.—We have arrived at our destination, and are located about three miles from Petersburg, and hope to-day to be able to make arrangements for the winter.

HEADQUARTERS ARMY NORTHERN VIRGINIA, 29th Dec., 1864.
Circular (Confidential.)

GENERAL: I desire that you will avail yourself of the present period of inactivity to re-organize and recruit the troops in your command as far as practicable.

Ascertain what regiments, if any, it would be advantageous to consolidate, and how such vacancies as may exist among the officers can best be filled. In every case in which you may think the officer to be promoted unsuitable for the new grade, you will forward a report as to his qualifications, in order that he may be brought before an examining board.

The difficulty of filling vacancies properly during active operations, and the importance of habituating the officers, who are to be promoted, to the duties of their new positions, render it proper that there should be no delay.

  Very respectfully,
   Your obedient servant,
    (Signed)   R. E. LEE, *Gen'l.*

Official:
 V. DABNEY, *A. A. Gen'l.*
 Brig. Gen. GRIMES, *Command'g Division.*

        6TH JANUARY, 1865

GEN. GRIMES:

 General Pickett has been directed to send one Brigade to the north side. This thins his line somewhat. You may have to move up to support him. He has been informed that should occasion require that he should have assistance, and should he request it of you, that you would be instructed to move up at once without waiting for orders from here. Please govern your action accordingly.

 By order of Gen. Lee:
  (Signed)   W. H. TAYLOR,
        A. A. G.

Brig. Gen. GRIMES, *Command'g Division.*

HEADQUARTERS PICKETT'S DIVISION, Jan. 7th, 1865.

GENERAL:

General Pickett has just received a telegram from General Lee stating that a Brigade from your Division has been ordered to relieve our right Brigade (Terry's) [*Tovey's crossed out*] early in the morning, so as to enable it to occupy the line formerly held by General Corse. The General desires me to say to you that great caution would have to be observed to prevent the movement of the troops from being seen from "the Tower;" that it will probably be best to delay relieving the picket until after dark to-morrow night. He advises that we send [*you send crossed out*] as large a Brigade as possible, as General Terry's [*Tovey's crossed out*] line at present covers a great deal of ground. He suggests also that the officer who relieves this Brigade had better see Colonel Flowree [*with "we" correction*], who is in command at this time, as early as possible in the morning, to make such arrangements as will most effectually secure the movements of the men from being observed by the enemy.

I am, General,

Very respectfully,

(Signed) E. R. BAIRD, *A. D. C.*

To Brig. Gen. B. GRIMES, *Command'g Division.*

HEADQUARTERS A. N. VA., Jan. 7th, 1865.

GENERAL:

General Lee bids me say that he wishes you tomorrow morning to move one of your Brigades to the position now occupied by General Pickett's right Brigade on the Bermuda Hundreds line.

His object is to relieve that Brigade, so that it can be moved to another point. You will find comfortable huts on the line, which the Brigade will occupy. In all military operations the commanding officer of the Brigade will report to General Pickett while on his line. General Gordon has been notified of this order.

I am, very respectfully,
Your obedient servant,
(Signed) C. S. VENABLE,
Lieut. Col. & A. D. C.

Brig. Gen. BRYAN GRIMES, *Command'g Division.*

HEADQUARTERS ARMY NORTHERN VIRGIANIA, 30th Jan., 1865.

Brig.-Gen. BRYAN GRIMES, *Commanding Division:*

GENERAL: The General Commanding desires you to have your Division prepared to move promptly in the morning should you receive orders to that effect.

Have everything in readiness to move without delay.

It may be necessary to send you to the north side of the James river.

    Very respectfully,
(Signed,)   W. H. TAYLOR, *A. A. G.*

       11 P. M., 5th February, 1865.
GEN. GRIMES:

The enemy's cavalry have not passed beyond Dinwiddie C. H. They advanced to that point and then retired.

The General says you need not go up the road. He wishes you to remain where you are, or near, any where near it. Your men can be made comfortable for the night. If they cannot be made comfortable, you will move down the Boydton plankroad until you can get to some wood. If you move, report your location when you halt.

    Respectfully,
(Signed,)   W. H. TAYLOR, *A. A. G.*

 HEADQUARTERS SECOND CORPS, Feb. 15th, 7 o'clock P. M.

COLONEL: The note from Gen. Ransom's Headquarters in relation to movement of troops is received. If there is an accumulation of force on this flank by the enemy with a view to serious move against the S. S. R. R. this weather may delay it, but I should be glad to have Grimes' Division keep in readiness to join me should the Commanding General think proper to have him report to me in case of a battle.

I am, Colonel,

Very respectfully,

(Signed,) J. B. GORDON,
Major-General Commanding.

To COL. TAYLOR, *A. A. G.*

[Endorsed as follows.]

GEN. GRIMES:

A movement of trains loaded with troops to the enemy's left was reported this evening, and you had better keep your Division prepared to move. Though it may not be necessary, it is advisable to be ready.

Very respectfully,

W. H. TAYLOR, *A. A. G.*

15th February, 1865.

[Further extracts from letters to his wife.]

February 15th.—Remained in camp near Petersburg until about the middle of the month. Request from Gen. Gordon to have Grimes' Division report to him in case of battle. Received my commission as Major-General 15th February, 1865.

Sutherland Depot, February 24th, 12 miles from Petersburg.—Left camp and came here as there was a prospect of a fight, but the heavy rains have delayed it.

February 28th.—Still at Sutherland's Depot. In accepting the appointment of Major-General, I hope I shall never bring discredit upon myself. The higher the position the more there is expected, and like all others who have done their duty in this war, have made enemies, but care little for them, provided I can perform my duties satisfactorily to my superior officers and for the good of the country.

Sutherland's Depot, March 1st.—Have been riding all day in order to learn the different roads in the surrounding country, and laying off new ones to enable me to move with rapidity to any point when my services may be required.

Sutherland's, March 2d.—Nothing of interest. Still stuck in the mud.

March 3d and 5th.—Roads still in such bad condition that they are almost impassable.

March 7th and 8th.—Still at Sutherland's. Had a serenade last night—the only thing to break the monotony. Weather still continues bad.

March 9th.—Still quiet.

March 10th.—This is the day set apart by the

President for thanksgiving and prayer, but the weather is so bad no service can be held out of doors.

March 12th.—Am worn out from fatigue and want of sleep. Received orders at 2 A. M. to leave for Dunlap's before daylight. At 4 A. M. began the march and upon nearly reaching the pontoon, received another dispatch countermanding the order. There was a rumor that Sheridan's raiders were moving on Richmond, and that caused the move.

Petersburg, March 14th, 1865.—Yesterday received orders to come to Petersburg and relieve Bushrod Johnson's Division, which I did, completing my march about 12 o'clock last night. Suffered terribly from sick nervous headache, attributed to a glass of wine I took at General Lee's, who noticed that I looked pale and fatigued, and recommended a glass of wine, and as this was something very unusual with him, concluded I would take it, and suffered in consequence.

This morning was up early examining everything on my line. Went to each picket post, and at some points so close you could almost see the whites of the Yankees' eyes. The Yankee lines are in full view, and at night there is constant firing between the pickets.

March 16th, 17th, 22d, 25th, Petersburg.—Telegraphed this morning of my welfare. This morning we charged the enemy's works and captured them, taking twelve to fifteen pieces of artillery, and a good many prisoners, but after taking their works they concentrated a large number of cannon upon us, besides several times our number of infantry and we were obliged to succumb after fighting two and a half hours, and retire to our breastworks. My loss was heavy, being 478 officers and men. Lieut. Barnes wounded. As usual I captured a horse to ride during the fight, as I could not get mine over the breastworks. It would have done your heart good to hear the men cheer as I rode up and down the line urging them to do their duty, but would to heaven this carnage was over and I permitted to retire from such scenes and live a quiet and domestic life.

Petersburg, March 27th.—Am well, trust you did not hear the report of my being killed. When Gen. Gordon saw me, he seemed very much surprised. Said he had just sent a flag of truce to recover my body, but I was pleased to know I had brought myself off safe.

March 28th.—Still at Petersburg.

March 29th, Petersburg.—Lieut. Barnes is doing

remarkably well. Gen. Cook had his arm badly broken and fears are entertained that it will have to be amputated.

March —. Our troops were to attack the enemy this morning at Burgen's Mills, and I trust that they may whip them. For once I am out of it, and not among the attacking party.

Confederate States of America,
WAR DEPARTMENT,
Richmond, June 1, 1864.

SIR:

You are hereby informed that the President, by and with the advice and consent of the Senate, has appointed you

Brigadier General

In the Provisional Army in the service of the Confederate States, to rank as such from the NINETEENTH day of MAY, one thousand eight hundred and sixty-four.

Immediately on receipt hereof please to communicate to this Department, through the Adjutant and Inspector General's office, your acceptance or non-acceptance of said appointment, and with your letter of acceptance return to the Adjutant and Inspector General the OATH herewith enclosed, properly filled up, subscribed and attested, reporting at the same time your Age, Residence, when appointed, and the State in which you were Born.

Should you accept, you will report for duty to Gen. R. E. Lee, to command late Daniel's Brigade.

JAMES A. SEDDON,
Secretary of War.

Brig. Gen. BRYAN GRIMES, *Comd'g, &c., P. A. C. S.*

HEADQUARTERS
DEPARTMENT NORTHERN VIRGINIA.

[Extract.]

SPECIAL ORDER
No. —.

III. Brigadier-General Bryan Grimes is assigned to the command of Daniel's old Brigade, Rodes' Division, 2nd Army Corps.

By command of Gen. R. E. Lee:

W. H. TAYLOR, *A. A. General.*

Brig. Gen. GRIMES, *Command'g, &c.*

Confederate States of America,

WAR DEPARTMENT,

Richmond, February 23d, 1865.

SIR:

You are hereby informed that the President, by and with the advice and consent of the Senate, has appointed you

Major-General,

In the Provisional Army in the service of the Confederate States, to rank as such from the Fifteenth day of February, one thousand eight hundred and sixty-five.

Immediately on receipt hereof please to communicate to this Department through the Adjutant and Inspector General's office your acceptance or non-acceptance of said appointment, and with your letter of acceptance return to the Adjutant and Inspector General the OATH, herewith enclosed, properly filled up, subscribed and attested, reporting at the same time your Age, Residence, when appointed, and the State in which you were Born.

Should you accept, you will report for duty to Gen. R. E. Lee to command the late Gen. Rodes' Division A. N. V.

JOHN C. BRECKENRIDGE,
Secretary of War.

Major-Gen. BRYAN GRIMES, *P. A. C. S.*

HEADQUARTERS
DEPARTMENT NORTHERN VIRGINIA.

[Extract.]

SPECIAL ORDER }
No. 55. }

XV. Major-General Bryan Grimes, P. A. C. S., is hereby assigned to the command of Rodes' old Division, 2nd Corps, and will report accordingly.

By command of Gen. R. E. Lee:

W. H. TAYLOR, *A. A. General.*

To Maj. Gen. BRYAN GRIMES, *Command'g, &c.*

Through Gen. GORDON.

NEAR WASHINGTON, N. C., Nov. 5th, 1879.
MAJOR JNO. W. MOORE,

Dear Sir: In compliance with your request, I herewith transmit my recollections of the circumstances attending the last days of the existence of the Army of Northern Virginia, embracing several days previous to the final surrender at Appomattox Court House.

On the night of Saturday, April 1, 1865, my Division occupied a portion of the defences around the city of Petersburg, my left resting on Otey's Battery, near the memorable Crater, my right extending to the dam on a creek beyond Battery 45, Ramseur's old Brigade of North Carolinians being commanded by Col. W. R. Cox, 2nd North Carolina, holding appointment as temporary Brigadier; on their right Archer's Brigade of Virginia Junior Reserves, Grimes' old Brigade of North Carolinians, commanded by Col. D. G. Cowand, of the 32d North Carolina, Battle's Brigade of Alabamians, commanded by Col. Hobson of 5th Alabama, Cook's Brigade of Georgians commanded by Col. Nash, extending to the left in the order above named, numbering for duty about 2,200 muskets, covering at least three and a half miles of the trenches around Petersburg, with one third of my men constantly on picket duty in our front, one third kept awake at the breastworks during the night, with one third only off duty at a time, and they required always to sleep with their accoutrements on and upon their arms, ready to repel an attack at a moment's warning.

About 10 o'clock on the night of April 1, 1865, the cannonading from the artillery and mortars in my front became unusually severe, and at about 11 o'clock the Federals charged, capturing my picket line, which consisted of pits dug in the earth for protection from sharp shooters, and occupied by my soldiers varying in distance from 150 to 300 yards in front of our main breastworks. I took measures immediately to re-establish this line, which was successfully accomplished, and our pits re-occupied. About daylight of the 2nd the enemy again drove in our pickets and charged Rune's salient at the point where Battle's Brigade was posted, carrying the works for a few hundred yards on each side of that point, doubling and throwing Cook's Brigade back a short distance. I hurried the commands of Cols. Cowand and Archer to the point of attack as rapidly as possible, charging the enemy who were in possession of and protected by our traverses and bomb proops (which were erected to prevent our line being enfiladed, and also as a place of refuge from their perpendicular mortar fire), and continued gradually to regain traverse after traverse of our captured works.

I then secured four pieces of artillery which were placed in our second line of works, whose services were invaluable in checking the advance of the enemy, thus confining them by grape and canister to this particular point at the salient, preventing their advancing to attack our lines in flank or rear ; Cook and Battle holding them in check on the left, and Cowand and Archer on the right of the captured works, their only point of egress being exposed to the fire of the artillery.

I regret my inability to recall the names and thus give honorable mention to those gallant artillerists who rendered me such effective service.

During the forenoon —— Brigade, under command of Col. ——, reported to me for duty and were placed near the artillery in this second line of earthworks (which had been constructed to fall back upon in case of disaster) to our first line. My dispositions were soon made to attack the enemy simultaneously at all points—Cowand and Archer on the right, Cook and Battle on the left, who were to drive them from the protection of their traverses. Col. —— commanded in front with a heavy line of skirmishers connecting his left with Cook and his right with Cowand. My four pieces of artillery poured grape and canister into the enemy, and I gave the signal for the infantry advance, when a general charge was made, but through a direct violation of orders on the part of Col. ——, this attack only partially succeeded, capturing that portion of the line alone upon which the skirmishers advanced, Col. —— having changed the direction of attack, and charged the point assigned to the skirmishers on the right, thereby leaving a space of three hundred yards unassailed. There is no doubt in my mind if Col. —— had attacked with vigor at that time, we could have driven the enemy entirely from our works. After the lapse of an hour, during which time the enemy were heavily reinforced, I ordered another attack from the second line in which Col. —— participated, but by again diverting his Brigade in the direction of Cowand's Brigade, instead of towards the salient, the enemy were dislodged from only a small portion of the lines.

Subsequently sixty men of Johnston's North Carolina Brigade, under command of Capt. Plato Durham, recaptured Fort Mahone, which for an hour had been so covered by our fire as to forbid their showing themselves. In taking this fort a large number of prisoners were captured; so many in fact, that when I first saw them skulking behind the earthworks for protection against the fire of their own men, I feared it was a ruse on the part of the enemy to surprise us, they having secreted themselves for safety in this work, and we in our charge had taken the only outlet.

After this no general attack was made, though we continued slowly but gradually to drive them from traverse to traverse.

About nightfall the enemy occupied some two hundred yards of our breastworks—through no inefficiency or negligence on the part of the officers and men were the works carried, but owing to the weakness of the line, its extreme length, and the want of sufficient force to defend it, for they acted most heroically on this trying occasion. Only one unwounded man (an officer) did I see seeking the rear, and he one whom I had the previous day ordered under arrest for trafficking with the enemy (exchanging tobacco for coffee). Him I hailed and inquired where he was going, when he recalled his arrest the previous day, from which I immediately released him and sent him back to his command.

I had a verbal conference with Gen. Lee and

afterwards officially reported my inability to hold this point against any vigorous attack. In consequence of this report, Lieut.-Col. Peyton, the Army Inspector, was sent the day before to examine this line, who coincided with my views and so reported to Gen. Lee. On an average throughout the space from man to man was at least eight feet in the line of trenches. I doubted not that with a reserve of five hundred men I could have driven the enemy from any point which they might capture, and repeatedly urged that such an arrangement be made, knowing well that the enemy by concentrating a large force on any given point could press their way through the line, and my only salvation was in having the means at hand of driving them back before large numbers could enter. Our left was the post of greatest danger, there should the reserve have been placed; but Gen. Lee informed me that every available man was on duty, and I must do the best I could.

On Sunday night of the 2nd we had orders to abandon the works, and without the knowledge of the Federals we withdrew to the north side of the Appomattox river, following the Hickory road to Goode's bridge, where we recrossed the Appomattox, proceeding towards Amelia C. H., which we reached on the morning of the fifth. Wednesday we remained stationary in line of battle, confronting the enemy until about dark, when we followed the army, bringing up the rear, being very much impeded on the march by the wagon train and its most miserable mismanagement, which, as I apprehended, would cause us some disaster. The enemy showed themselves on Thursday about 8 o'clock A. M. in our rear and on our left flank when near Amelia Springs, and in a short time began to press us vigorously.

I then formed Cox's and Cowand's Brigades in line of battle, with a heavy skirmish line in front to impede their progress and to cover our rear, sending Battle's, Cook's and Archer's Brigades forward for one half mile to form there, across the road, in line of battle, in order to allow Cowand and Cox to retreat safely when the enemy had deployed and prepared to attack; our right flank being protected by a North Carolina Brigade of cavalry under General Roberts. In this manner alternating the Brigades throughout the day we continued to oppose the enemy and retreat, endeavoring to protect the lagging wagon train, which was successfully done up to about 4 o'clock P. M., when we approached Sailor's Creek, and upon the ridge running parallel with that stream we made the final stand of the day, the wagons becoming blocked up at the bridge crossing this stream. At this point Gen. Lee ordered me if possible to hold this line of hills until he could have artillery put in position on the opposite hills over the creek parallel with those I occupied.

The enemy pushed on rapidly, attacking us with very great pertinacity. We here repeatedly repulsed their assaults, but by turning both of our flanks they succeeded in not only dislodging but driving us across the creek in confusion. About now the artillery from the heights, occupied by Gen. Lee, opened upon the enemy, and the sun being down they did not cross the creek. After we broke, personally I was so pressed that the space between the two wings of the enemy was not over two hundred yards when I sought safety in retreat. I galloped to the creek (the bridge being in their possession) where the banks were very precipitous, and for protection from their murderous fire concluded to jump my horse in, riding him through the water and effect my escape by abandoning him on the other side, the bullets of the enemy whistling around me like hail all the while. By great good fortune the opposite banks proving not so precipitous and my horse seeming to appreciate the situation, clambered up the height, starting off in a run, thus securing my safety. This same animal, Warren, I still own and treasure for his past services. That night we took the road for Farmville, crossing the Appomattox at High Bridge, posting guards at the south side, thus collecting all stragglers and returning them to their commands.

The next morning (Friday) we continued our march down the railroad and formed line of battle on the Lynchburg road, still endeavoring to preserve that "impediment of Cæsar's"—the wagon train—marching by the left flank through the woods parallel to the road traveled by the wagon train, and about one hundred or so yards distant from the road. Upon reaching the road and point that turns towards Lynchburg from the Cumberland road, three of my Brigades, Cook's, Cox's and Cowand's, had crossed the Cumberland road and were in line of battle, and at right angles with Battle's and Archer's Brigades, who were still parallel with the Cumberland road. Heavy firing was going on at this point, when Gen. Mahone came rushing up and reported that the enemy had charged, turning his flank, and driving his men from their guns and the works which he had erected early in the day for the protection of these cross roads. I then ordered my three Brigades, Cook's, Cox's and Cowand's at a doublequick on the line, with Battle and Archer, charging the enemy and driving them well off from Mahone's works, recapturing the artillery taken by them and capturing a large number of prisoners and holding this position until sent for by Gen. Lee, who complimented the troops of the Division upon the charge made and the service rendered, ordering me to leave a skirmish line in my front and that Fields' Division would occupy my position, I to hurry with all possible dispatch to the road which intersected the Lynchburg road, as the enemy's cavalry were reported to be approaching by that road.

We reached this road, halting and keeping the enemy in check until the wagons had passed, and then continued the march parallel with the road travelled by the wagon train, continuing thus to march until night, when we took the road following to protect the trains.

On Saturday the 8th no enemy appeared, and we marched undisturbed all day. Up to this time since the evacuation of Petersburg we had marched day and night, continually followed and harrassed by the enemy. The men were very much jaded and suffering for necessary sustenance, our halts not having been sufficiently long to prepare their food, besides all of our cooking utensils not captured or abandoned were where we could not reach them. This day Bushrod Johnson's Division was assigned to and placed under my command by order of Gen. Lee. Upon passing a clear stream of water and learning that the other Division of the Corps had gone into camp some two or three miles ahead, I concluded to halt and give my broken down men an opportunity to close up and rejoin us, and sent a message to Gen. Gordon, commanding the Corps, making known my whereabouts, informing him I would be at any point he might designate at any hour desired.

By dark my men were all quiet and asleep. About nine o'clock I heard the roar of artillery in our front and in consequence of information received I had my command aroused in time and passed through the town of Appomattox C. H. before daylight, where, upon the opposite side of the town, I found the enemy in my front. Throwing out my skirmishers and forming line of battle, I reconnoitered and satisfied myself as to their position, and awaited the arrival of Gen. Gordon for instructions, who awhile before day, accompanied by Gen. Fitz. Lee, came to my position when we held a council of war. Gen. Gordon was of the opinion that the troops in our front were cavalry and Gen. Fitz Lee should attack. Fitz Lee thought they were infantry and that Gordon should attack. They discussed the matter so long that I became impatient, and said it was some one's duty to attack, and that immediately, and I felt satisfied that they could be driven from cross roads occupied by them, which was the route it was desirable our wagon train should pursue, and that I would undertake it; whereupon Gordon said, "Well, drive them off." I replied, "I cannot do it with my Division alone, but require assistance. He then said, " You can take the other two Divisions of the Corps." About this time it was becoming sufficiently light to make the surrounding localities visible. I then rode down and invited Gen. Walker, who commanded a Division on my left composed principally of Virginians, to ride with me, showing him the position of the enemy and explaining to him my views and plan of attack. He agreed with me as to its advisability. I did this because I felt I had assumed a very great responsibility when I took upon myself the charge of making the attack. I then made dispositions to dislodge the Federals from their position, placing Bushrod Johnson's Division upon my right, with instructions to attack and take the enemy in flank, while my Division skirmishers charged in front where temporary earthworks had been thrown up by the enemy their cavalry holding the crossings of the road with a battery. I soon perceived a disposition on their part to attack this Division in flank. I rode back and threw their right so as to take advantage of some ditches and fences to obstruct the cavalry if they should attempt to make a charge. In the meantime the cavalry of Fitz Lee were proceeding by a circuitous route to get in rear of them at these cross roads. The enemy observing me placing these troops in position fired upon me with four pieces of artillery. I remember well the appearance of the shell, and how directly they came towards me, exploding, and completely enveloping me in smoke. I then gave the signal to advance, at the same time Fitz Lee charged those posted at the cross roads, when my skirmishers attacked the breastworks which were taken without much loss on my part, also capturing several pieces of artillery and a large number of prisoners, I at the same time moving the Division up to the support of the skirmishers in echelon by Brigades, driving the enmy in confusion for three quarters of a mile beyond a range of hills covered with oak undergrowth. I then learned from prisoners that my right flank was threat ͝ ed. Halting my troops I placed the skirmishers, commanded by Col. J. R. Winston, 45th N. C. Troops, in front about one hundred yards distant, to give notice of indication of attack. Placed Cox's Brigade, which occupied the right of the Division at right angles to the other troops to watch that flank. The other Divisions of the Corps (Walker and Evans) were on the left. I then sent an officer to Gen. Gordon announcing our success and that the Lynchburg road was open for the escape of the wagons, and that I awaited orders. Thereupon I received an order to withdraw, which I declined to do, supposing that Gen. Gordon did not understand the commanding position which my troops occupied. He continued to send me order after order to the same effect which I still disregarded, being under the impression that he did not cemprehend our favorable location, until finally I received a message from him with an additional one as coming from Gen. Lee to fall back. I felt the difficulty of withdrawal without disaster, and ordered Col. J. R. Winston, commanding the skirmish line which had been posted in my front on reaching first these hills, to conform his movements to those of the Division, and to move by the left flank so as to give us notice of an attack from that quarter. I then ordered Cox to maintain his position in line of battle, and not to show himself until our rear was 100 yards distant, and then to fall back in line of battle, so as to protect our rear and right flank from assault. I then instructed Major Peyton, of my staff, to start the left in motion, and I continued with the rear.

The enemy, upon seeing us move off, rushed out from under cover with a cheer, when Cox's Brigade, lying concealed at the brow of a hill, rose and fired a volley into them, which drove them back into the woods, the Brigade then following their retreating comrades in line of battle unmolested. After proceeding about half the distance to the position occupied by us in the morning, a dense mass of the enemy in column (Infantry) appeared on our right, and advanced without firing towards the earthworks captured by us in the early morning, when a Battery of our artillery opened with grape and cannister, and drove them under the shelter of the woods.

As my troops approached their position of the morning, I rode up to General Gordon and asked where I should form line of battle. He replied, "Anywhere you choose." Struck by the strangeness of the reply, I asked an explanation, whereupon he informed me that we would be surrendered. I expressed very forcibly my dissent to being surrendered, and indignantly upbraided him for not giving me notice of such intention, as I could have escaped with my Division and joined Gen. Joe Johnston, then in North Carolina. Furthermore, that I should then inform my men of the purpose to surrender, and that whomsoever desired to escape that calamity could go with me, and galloped off to carry this idea into effect. Before reaching my troops, however, General Gordon overtook me, and placing his hand on my shoulder, asked me if I were going to desert the army, and tarnish my own honor as a soldier; that it would be a reflection upon General Lee, and an indelible disgrace to me, that I, an officer of rank, should escape under a flag of truce, which was then pending. I was in a dilemma, and knew not what to do, but finally concluded to say nothing on the subject to my troops.

Upon reaching them, one of the soldiers inquired if General Lee had surrendered, and upon answering I feared it was a fact that we had been surrendered, he cast away his musket, and holding his hands aloft, cried in an agonized voice, "Blow, Gabriel, blow! My God, let him blow, I am ready to die!" We then went beyond the creek at Appomattox Court House, stacked arms amid the bitter tears of bronzed veterans regretting the necessity of capitulation.

Among the incidents, ever fresh in my memory, of this fatal day to the Confederacy, is the remark of a private soldier. When riding up to my old regiment to shake by the hand each comrade who had followed me through four years of suffering, toil, and privation often worse than death, to bid them a final affectionate, and, in many instances, an eternal farewell, a' cadaverous, ragged, barefooted man, grasped me by the hand, and choking with sobs, said: "Good-bye, General; God bless you, we will go home, make three more crops, and try them again." I mention this instance simply to show the spirit, the pluck, and the faith of our men in the justice of our cause, and that he surrendered more to grim famine than to the prowess of our enemies.

That day, and the next, the terms of surrender were adjusted: the following day our paroles signed and countersigned; and on Wednesday, April 12th, 1865, we stacked arms in an old field, and each man sought his home as best he might.

I have given in the above a simple, true, and unvarnished statement of facts, occurring during the dying struggles of the Army of Northern Virginia, in so far, only as I was an eye-witness and participant in those events; with no view to laud my own achievements, or seeming to seek an undeserved honor, or to take the least sprig of laurel from another's brow, but simply in the interest of the truth of history.

I assert that I was at Appomattox, and that I commanded my own Division at Appomattox; and General Gordon, the Corps commander, bears me out in this assertion, and, moreover, states that I volunteered my services, and did make the last charge made by the Infantry at Appomattox.

Very respectfully,
Your obedient servant,
BRYAN GRIMES,
Major-General in late P. A. C. S.

RALEIGH, N. C., December 20th, 1879.

To Gen. BRYAN GRIMES,

My Dear Sir: I owe you a thousand thanks for your full and extremely valuable letter. It explains many things I did not understand before, and will greatly add to the vindication of the North Carolinians as to the last sad hours of the Army of Northern Virginia. Pray excuse my delay in acknowledging your great kindness, and believe me,

Very truly yours,
(Signed) J. W. MOORE.

General Grimes' Reply to Letter of Chas. C. Jones, Jr., April 16, 1872.

Accept my sincere thanks for your book, and although as you say local in its character, have derived great pleasure from perusal. The mention of Gen. Colquitt's name recalled some associations with it. One was that upon reaching Yorktown, April 9th, (1862,) we relieved the sixth Georgia Regiment and established ourselves in Col. Colquitt's "hole in the ground" with a tent over it, and in a few days found one of the attendants of close quarters, and my person covered before we ever dreamed of such pests. Another reminiscence is having a Bible (in my library now) picked up on the night of our retreat from Yorktown, I having been detailed to bring off the pickets. I enclose you autographs of Generals Ramseur and Daniel, with his approval upon application for leave of absence while near Orange Court House; also a paper addressed to Col. Taylor, I suppose upon which I made this application. I have fragments and skeletons of reports made of different engagements—Gettysburg, last few days of the war, from breaking of our lines at Petersburg to the morning of surrender at Appomattox Court House, and some others. The last infantry charge by the Army of Northern Virginia was made by my

Division, as General Gordon, our Corps commander, will substantiate. The form of parole for General Johnston's troops was taken from my papers, borrowed by Col. Wherry, Gen. Schofield's Adjutant General or Aid-de-Camp, to guide Schofield in adjusting this matter. By-the-by, Generals Sherman, Schofield, Terry, Bevis, *et id omne genus*, had a champagne drinking in Raleigh just after Johnston's surrender, and sent this same Col. Wherry over, to invite me to join them, which I most indignantly declined. That evening we heard of Lincoln's assassination. Reminiscences of the past crowd upon me, and however pleasant, or rather unpleasant, may not prove agreeable to you, and if I do not halt will exhaust my paper before I have given you information asked for. You can procure all information relative to General Ramseur from Capt. Richmond, (Aid-de-Camp to Gen. R.,) Milton, N. C. I wrote to Mr. Richmond a few weeks ago, and received no reply. If you do not hear from him, then address Hon. D. Schenck, Lincolnton, N. C., who married Gen. R.'s sister. Ramseur married his first cousin (Richmond's sister). Hon. E. Conigland, Halifax, N. C., will cheerfully give you all information relative to his brother-in-law, General Daniel. William E. Anderson, President Citizens National Bank, Raleigh, can tell you everything about his brother, Gen. G. B. Anderson. You ask nothing of my dear friends and relatives, J. J. Pettigrew and L. O'B. Branch, the first killed at Falling Waters upon the retreat from Pennsylvania, the latter killed at Sharpsburg. You perhaps regard Pettigrew as a South Carolinian. We claim him. He is a native, and was educated in the State, was Colonel of a North Carolina Regiment, and commanded a North Carolina Brigade at time of his death. Rev. W. S. Pettigrew, Henderson, N. C., will give you all particulars relative to him, and Mrs. L. O'B. Branch, Raleigh, or son W. A. B. Branch, Washington, N. C., will take pleasure in communicating all facts relative to Gen. Branch. There is Gen. Pender whose widow and brother live in Tarboro, N. C. Pender I knew but slightly, only after the war commenced, the others were life-long acquaintances and friends from childhood. I think it probable I shall revisit New York on the 4th or 5th of May and stop at the St. Nicholas. I can, if of service to you, send you a roster of all the Regiments and field officers from North Carolina.

  Very respectfully yours,
    BRYAN GRIMES.

[Letter from Gen. J. B. Gordon.]

NEW YORK, May 6th, 1872.

Gen. BRYAN GRIMES, *N. C.:*

MY DEAR GENERAL: Yours asking my recollection of the participation of your Division in the last day's battle at Appomattox C. H. would have been answered before I left my home in Georgia, but for circumstances beyond my control. It is a source of pleasure to me not only to do this but also to express my sincere appreciation of your valuable services during that portion of the war when it was my fortune to command the 2nd Corps Army Northern Virginia, to which your Division was attached. When I was first placed in command of the Corps in the Fall of 1864 at or near Petersburg, you will remember that you were detached from the other Divisions and did not join them until a short time before the attack upon Gen. Grant's lines in front of Petersburg. You participated in the battles then and during the terrible days and nights which followed prior to and after the breaking of our lines by Grant's army, as well as upon the retreat. But it is of the last fight of the army of Northern Virginia in which you bore so *conspicuous* a part at Appomattox C. H. that you ask my recollections. It would be difficult, my dear General, to forget your anxiety to get your Division well up and compact on the evening of the 8th of April, the day preceding that last battle and the final surrender of the army, as well as your assurance to me that if allowed to rest and gather up your broken down men, you would be on hand at any time during the night of the 8th or morning of the 9th, to take part in any movement which might be ordered. My consent you will remember was obtained that you should go into camp and rest your men, but before day on the morning of the 9th of April, you were at the front ready to participate with your Division in the last effort ever to be made by the army of Gen. Lee.

The plan agreed upon at the counsel of war held at Gen. Lee's Headquarters during the night of the 8th between Gen. Lee, Gen. Pendleton commanding the artillery, Gen. Fitz Hugh Lee commanding the cavalry, Gen. Longstreet and myself who commanded the two wings of his army, was this: My command, consisting of about one half of the army, with the cavalry, was to attack the enemy's cavalry in front of Appomattox C. H., and attempt to cut a way out, and Longstreet and the artillery not engaged with my command and the wagon train, was to follow. It was supposed that nothing more than the enemy's cavalry was in our front, and though largely outnumbering the whole of my command and the cavalry of Gen. Lee, yet it was supposed, as the result proved, that Sheridan's cavalry could be beaten back. It was during the preparation for this final move in the early morning of the 9th, that you offered to make the attack in front.

Your Division with the other troops were placed in line while Gen. Fitz Hugh Lee's cavalry moved to our right. The attack was made and proved eminently successful, resulting in the capture of the enemy's works which he had temporarily thrown up in our front, and the taking of six pieces (I think) of his artillery. You were not halted for a considerable time but pressed steadily forward to the front, until I ordered you to rear, upon receiving intelligence from Gen. R. E. Lee that a flag of truce was in existence between himself and Gen. Grant, and upon the appearance and advance of heavy bodies of infantry upon both our flanks. Your indisposition to retreat then, and your anxiety to go on, was manifest ; but I knew more of the situation than you did, and in accordance with the understanding at the counsel of war the night previous, the appearance of these large bodies of the enemy's infantry, and the impossibility of Gen. Longstreet's moving up, the constantly increasing distance between us, and the pressing of the enemy's force into this space, it was necessary for me to notify Gen. Lee of the situation then, and these circumstances rendered resistance for any positive advantage useless, and loss of life by our brave men of no avail.

On the receipt of the note from Gen. Lee I ordered you to the rear, and notified Gen. Sheridan of the existence of a " Flag of Truce," who insisted upon the separate surrender of my command to him, which I refused. It was at this time you asked me what the meaning was of my instructions to you to put your men in any position you could select, and suggested that I permit you to return to the front. It was very painful to announce to you and to the troops the surrender of the army, and when you were made aware of it, you expressed your regret that I had not informed you while you were in front, that you might have made the effort to escape with your command.

I was touched, General, by your indisposition to meet this dreaded ordeal, as I was by the grief, the anguish of all our brave men, but it was all over—all was done that could be done by the army, and any escape of small bodies of troops would have been charged as treachery on Gen. Lee's part toward Gen. Grant, from whose overwhelming forces it was impossible now to extricate the remnant of the "Army of Northern Virginia." This occasion was the most trying one of all our lives; but, General, the ungenerous effort to humiliate us since the war, by the strong arm of power, has made upon my heart, and doubtless upon yours, a more ineffaceable impression than all else connected with our past history. We were entitled to honorable, magnanimous legislation by the General Government; but the purposes of the party in power have seemed to be only to irritate by proscriptive laws, and drive us to desperation by the support of those forced in power over us, who in the name of Law have *robbed* us, in the name of Liberty have inaugurated the rule of the Bayonet, arrested and imprisoned the innocent, and gloated in the oppression of our citizens.

May the God of Righteousness bring us deliverance.

Most truly your friend,
(Signed) J. B. GORDON.
Major-Gen. GRIMES, *N. C.*

On page 95 of Col. Walter H. Taylor's book entitled "Four Years with General Lee," (which book is now in Gen. Grimes' library,) the first section is marked thus ‡ and reads as follows:

"General Lee witnessed the flight of the Federals through Gettysburg and up the hills beyond. He then directed me to go to General Ewell and to say to him, that from the position which he occupied he could see the enemy retreating over those hills without organization and in great confusion, that it was only necessary to press "those people" in order to secure possession of the heights, and that, if possible, he wished him to do this. In obedience to these instructions, I proceeded immediately to General Ewell and delivered the order of General Lee; and after receiving from him some message for the commanding general in regard to the prisoners captured, returned to the latter and reported that his order had been delivered."

All around the margin of this page appears the following in pencil, and written in Gen. Grimes' own handwriting:

"I was in the lead and saw the first pieces of artillery, two in number, making for this hill. The enemy were routed and retreating in great confusion. Gen. Ramseur, with my regiment in advance, were rushing up, and following the enemy, and without the slightest doubt in my mind, could have captured these guns and occupied the hill, but an officer of rank rode up and advised that we await reinforcements, which was done, and we were drawn back to the main street of Gettysburg, and there remained, without firing a shot the whole evening—several hours of daylight."

Gen. Ramseur says in his report of the battle of Gettysburg, (see Southern Historical Papers.—C.):

"The enemy was pushed through Gettysburg to the heights beyond, when I received an order to halt and form line of battle in a street in Gettysburg running east and west.

"To Colonel Parker, 30th North Carolina; Colonel Bennett, 19th North Carolina; Colonel Grimes, 4th North Carolina, and Major Hurt, 2nd North Crrolina, my thanks are due for skill and gallantry displayed by them in this day's fight."

General Grimes received a copy of Moore's History of North Carolina only a few days before his death, and had but little opportunity to examine it, and had only read disconnected parts of it.

On page 170, Vol. II, in the two last lines of said page he makes the following corrections: Erases "Twelfth, Colonel Daniel," and writes, " Fourteenth,

Col. R. T. Bennett ;" and erases " Twentieth, Col. T.
F. Toon," and writes " Thirty-seventh, Col. F. M.
Parker."

On page 190, Vol. II, on the left margin of said
page, appears the following written also in pencil in
his own handwriting :

" I commanded Anderson's Brigade at this battle, consisting of the 2nd, 4th, 14th and 30th Regiments of N. C. Troops. BRYAN GRIMES."

On page 259, Vol. II, Major Moore in describing
Gen. Lee leading the charge in person at the battle
of Spottsylvania C. H., places the date of this charge
in person by Gen. Lee on the morning of the 10th
of May.

On the right margin of said page is written in
pencil : " It was on the 5th May that Gen. Lee led
the charge in person."

On page 260, Vol. II, Major Moore says: "Conspicuous in this charge was the youthful and slender
form of Brigadier-General Stephen D. Ramseur, of
Lincoln county, North Carolina." On the left margin of said page is written in pencil : " This charge
was led by Col. Bryan Grimes, commanding Ramseur's Brigade, Ramseur being disabled by a wound."

[About the time the printing of this book was nearly completed the following was found in a book in Gen. Grimes' library, in his own handwriting, and is given here exactly as it is written.—C.]

Ewell's Corps, composed of Rodes, Early and Johnson's commands, surprised Gen. Milroy. We drove the enemy's cavalry from the summit, and ousted them to intercept the retreat of the enemy from Winchester. Captured the cavalry camp at Berryville. We moved down to Martinsburg and drove the enemy into and through the town, taking several pieces of artillery and 700 prisoners. Then moved up and crossed the Potomac river at Williamsport. Occupied Chambersburg on 23rd of June, 1863. Was Provost Marshal of Hagerstown. There we spent several days, and then moved to Chambersburg. Insidious talk of man of Company A: turned him over to his own men for punishment. Sent to Carlisle within eight miles of Harrisburg on picket duty. Headquarters in brick house. Woman's remark about Quartermaster. Regiment quartered in a very large house. Saw the Perry militia coming out with their high sugar-loaf hats. Put a portion of my picket in ambush, allowing militia to pass, susprising them in front, and shooting in their rear. Supplied my men with their hats, which fell off in their confusion. Their stampede through

Harrisburg, through the wheat fields. Here tasted for the first time Plantation Bitters, taken from the pocket of a dead Federal. We stampeded all of them, about 500. Killed and wounded many. Captured many horses without having a man wounded. Were nearer Harrisburg than perhaps any troops except cavalry scouts. Severity of orders against plundering the inhabitants. Punishment of men who went in a house and took jewelry. The rest of our Brigade occupied the U. S. Barracks. Move towards Gettysburg. Rode in ambulance all the time, except when expecting an engagement, owing to injury on my foot.

ERRATA.

Page 1, line 16, should read, "as far as he had executed it."

Page 10, line 7, should read, "were repeated" in place of "wires repeated."

Page 15, line 4, should read, "pinned" instead of "penned."

Page 52, line 22, should read, "which broke and ran" for "who broke and run."

Page 67, line 21, should read, "Capt. Stitt" instead of "Still."

Page 67, line 23, should read, "one of my couriers (Sherwood Badger.)"

Page 68, line 18, should read, "Capt. Stitt" instead of "Still."

Page 72, line 13, should read, "able to hobble along" instead of "unable," &c.

Page 80, line 16, should read, "march" for "March."

Page 117, line 6, should read, "Divisions" for "Division."

There are a few typographical errors which will readily suggest themselves to the reader.

www.ingramcontent.com/pod-product-compliance
Lightning Source LLC
Chambersburg PA
CBHW022131160426
43197CB00009B/1241